Instant Library Lessons

Kindergarten

Karen A. Farmer Wanamaker

UpstartBooks

Fort Atkinson, Wisconsin

To J. E. Woodard Elementary School, Columbia, TN
1990–1999
Creativity can survive in isolation,
but it can only thrive within a creative community.

Published by UpstartBooks
W5527 State Road 106
P.O. Box 800
Fort Atkinson, Wisconsin 53538-0800
1-800-448-4887

© Karen A. Farmer Wanamaker, 2005
Cover design and illustrations by Debra Sletten

The paper used in this publication meets the minimum requirements of
American National Standard for Information Sciences —
Permanence of Paper for Printed Library Materials. ANSI/NISO Z39.48-1992.

Contents

 Introduction

When I was in college preparing to become a Library Media Specialist, I had no idea how important my experiences with and love for designing curriculum would become. Once I reached the real world I quickly realized that everyone in an elementary school had text-books, workbooks, teachers' editions, or at the very least, a list of objectives—everyone, that is, except the Library Media Specialist.

Through the years I searched for a source of lesson plans that provided for the needs of Library Media Specialists and their students. In the meantime I created my own lessons. This was actually a plus as I truly enjoyed the creative process. Unfortunately, there was never enough time to fully develop the lesson ideas with all that had to be done in the library. Now I have the opportunity to do what I always thought someone ought to do. This book is designed to provide a year's worth of lessons—all that is needed are the suggested books and the children.

These lessons were specifically designed to support the following educational beliefs:

- Instruction should include exposure to fiction and nonfiction at all levels.

- Learning experiences are most successful when taught in a consistent frame that moves learning from whole class instruction through teamwork and working in pairs before expecting children to work alone.

- In order for students to have the best opportunity to learn, adults should foster higher levels of thinking by asking questions that encourage thought and by teaching students to ask their own thought-provoking questions.

- Using children's literature to direct learning is most appropriate when addressing library instruction.

- Interactive instruction based on what is known about learning styles provides the best environment for learning.

- Library instruction should fully support the school-wide curriculum.

How to Use This Book

The length and number of library sessions varies greatly from library to library, and often from school year to school year within the same location. Many other factors, such as the number of students per class and the amount of checkout time needed, contribute to the amount of instructional time available in a library.

For these reasons, this book was designed to provide 36 one-hour lessons. Each lesson can be used in one session or broken into smaller segments for multiple sessions. These lessons offer Library Media Specialists choices in determining the makeup of their particular library class instruction.

The Instant Library Lessons series includes Lesson Learning Ideas that encompass the following instructional strands:

- **Library Skills:** Including, but not limited to, research and learning skills.

- **Literature Appreciation:** Exposure to and experience with a variety of print genres.

- **Techniques of Learning:** Strategies such as questioning skills and interactive learning that support lifelong learning.

- **Comprehension:** Developing learning processes that support effective readers and learners.

- **Writing Experiences:** Fostering the link between reading and writing needed throughout a lifetime.

- **Oral Language:** Opportunities to develop and refine skills in interpersonal communication from speaking, listening and viewing.

Each individual lesson includes:

- **Featured Book(s).** The book or books the lesson is based upon with corresponding summary information.

- **Lesson Learning Ideas.** Specific lesson objectives based on the instructional strands developed for Instant Library Lessons. See pages 12–14.

- **Materials.** Items to be collected prior to instruction. Ordering information is available (see pages 187–189 for details) so the needed items can be obtained as easily as possible.

- **Before Class.** A list of tasks to complete before teaching the lesson.

- **Lesson Plan.** Presented in a format that can be followed step by step or altered to meet your specific needs.

Suggested Library Set-Up

In order to fully implement all of the lesson ideas included in this book a sample room layout has been created (see page 11). Recommendations include:

- Library furniture that includes enough tables and chairs to accommodate all of the students from one class within a given area. Each table should have a permanent container (basket) with crayons or markers, scissors and glue. Additional items, such as books or lesson materials, can be added when necessary. A permanent table sign label will assist in giving directions to students.

- A gathering area that provides for a more intimate sharing of books and learning experiences. The gathering area will need a stool or chair for the librarian. The students can sit on the floor. A big book stand, overhead projector on a movable cart, screen, easel with chart paper or chalkboard, TV with VCR and/or DVD complete the needed equipment.

- Other items which help organize the library setting might include: a movable book return cart located near the library entrance; a movable cart or table for a container of shelf markers and to display check-out name cards in divided containers; and a place for free reading materials (this could be a section within existing book shelves and/or a table space and should have enough room to accommodate a laundry-sized basket and several smaller baskets).

Tips of the Trade

- **Ready Rhyme.** Whenever students are seated on the floor, teach them this rhyme to help them learn how to get ready to listen. You can use the sign language words provided to go with the rhyme. Repeat the rhyme with motions until all of the students are ready.

    If you are seated on your bottom, *(Sit)*
    With your legs crossed,
    And your eyes this way, *(Look)*
    You're ready, *(Ready)*
    You're ready,
    You're ready,
    Yea.

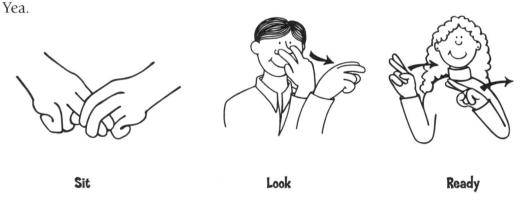

Sit   **Look**   **Ready**

- When you need to get your children's attention, teach them these words in sign language:

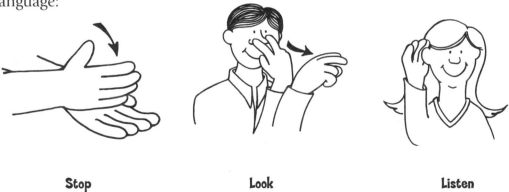

Stop   **Look**   **Listen**

Do not continue until every student is participating in the signing.

- When it is time for students to line up to leave the library call one table at a time. This can be done by labeling each table with a different color table sign label. Then use sign language or a foreign language to instruct the students when it is their turn. For example, say and/or sign the following phrase:

Red Table, line up slowly and quietly.

Then, continue with yellow, green, blue, black, white, purple, orange or whatever colors you choose. Use one of the following Web sites to locate sign language information: *www.handspeak.com* or *www.mastertech-home.com/ASLDict.html*.

- In order to get a line of children all going in the same direction teach them to "ENT." (If your eyes, ears, nose and throat are facing the door you are ready to go!)

- **Wiggle Squeezers.** Often during instruction students will need to take a break. Use one or more of the following movement activities to provide a break.

Shake Your Sillies Out

<u>Verse 1</u>: *(Hold hands slightly above waist level with elbows bent at 90 degree angle. Rotate arms and hips from side to side in a twisting motion. On the last line of the verse, point index fingers while moving hands up and down at the wrist.)*
You've got to shake, shake, shake your sillies out.
Shake, shake, shake your sillies out.
Shake, shake, shake your sillies out.
And wiggle your waggles away.

<u>Verse 2</u>: Clap your crazies out. *(Clap hands on first three lines. On the last line of the verse, point index fingers while moving hands up and down at the wrist.)*

<u>Verse 3</u>: Stretch your stretchies out. *(Stretch arms in various directions on the first three lines. On the last line of the verse, point index fingers while moving hands up and down at the wrist.)*

<u>Verse 4</u>: Jump your jingles out. *(Jump up and down in place on the first three lines of the rhyme. On the last line of the verse, point index fingers while moving hands up and down at the wrist.)*

<u>Verse 5</u>: Yawn your yuckies out. *(Slow down the pace of the chant and speak softly during this verse. On the first three lines cover your mouth and yawn while inhaling during the word "yawn." On the last line of the verse, point index fingers while moving hands up and down at the wrist.)*

Hi, My Name is Joe

Hi, my name is Joe.
I've got a wife and three kids,
And I work in a button factory.
One day the boss came in,
He said, "Joe, are you busy?"
I said, "No."
He said, "Do it like this."

The first time just say the words. Then add a motion and repeat the words again while doing the motion. At the end of each verse, add an additional movement while continuing each of the previous movements.

Suggested movements: *Wave right hand; wave left hand; raise and lower one foot; march in place by raising and lowering each foot one at a time; and nod head. On the last verse change the words to: Joe, are you busy? I said, yes!*

Oliver Twist

Oliver, twist, twist, twist,
(Place your hands on your hips and twist side to side each time you say "twist.")
Can't do this, this, this, *(Stretch both arms high over head.)*
Touch your toes, toes, toes, *(Bend at the waist and touch your fingers to your toes.)*
Nobody nose, nose, nose.
(Place your right hand into your left palm and touch your nose with both hands.)

Say the rhyme three times, repeating it faster each time. Then do the rhyme one last time in extra slow motion to calm the children down.

Do Your Ears Hang Low?

Do your ears hang low? *(Backs of hands on ears, fingers down.)*
Do they wobble to and fro? *(Sway fingers.)*
Can you tie 'em in a knot? *(Tie large knot in air.)*
Can you tie 'em in a bow? *(Draw bow in air with both hands.)*
Can you throw 'em over your shoulder, *(Throw both hands over left shoulder.)*
Like a continental soldier? *(Salute.)*
Do your ears hang low? *(Backs of hands on ears, fingers down.)*

Always do the last verse in extra slow motion to calm the children down and prepare them to return to work.

- **Free Reading Area.** Throughout the lessons there are suggested materials for the "Free Reading Area." Note the map under suggested library set-up to see where to locate such materials. These are self-directed materials students can use when they have wait time. Wait time most often occurs during check out since all children can't select a book at the same time. Establish guidelines for using the materials within your library. Be sure to introduce and practice how to use the materials before they appear in the Free Reading Area.

Materials for a free reading area might include:

- Velcro boards, aprons and mitts with story pieces in plastic bags based on Literature Pictures

- metal boards with story pieces in plastic bags based on Literature Pictures

- minute books—brief, paperback books for early readers

- children's magazines

Add items as recommended in the lesson plans. Rotate items so students don't get bored with the offerings. House similar items in plastic baskets for easy access and clean up.

Literature Pictures (LPs)

Literature Pictures work well for presentations and Free Reading Area materials.

1. Make copies of the pictures.

2. Color the pictures. If coloring anything the size of your hand or smaller, it should be colored with the thick lead, colored art pencils. These can be found in art stores (Hobby Lobby or Michael's) or some school supply stores and catalogs. The brand that has been most successful is Prismacolor. If enlarging the pictures so they are larger than your hand, artist pastel chalks work well. After coloring, lightly spray the pictures with cheap hairspray. Most of the pastels found in school and art supply stores are fine for this activity.

3. Back each piece with poster board. Use spray glue, which is often called spray adhesive. This makes for a smooth finish and can be bought at paint and discount stores. Cut out the pieces.

4. Write any cues needed for telling the story on the back of the individual pieces. Then laminate and cut out the pieces.

5. Decide between making the story into a Velcro apron story or a metal board presentation. For an apron version, back the pieces with adhesive-backed Velcro but also glue them with Tacky glue. For a metal board story, use the adhesive-backed magnetic strips and Tacky glue.

Library Table Signs

1. Decide how to identify tables (by colors, numbers, letters or pictures). Instant Library Lessons uses colors.

2. Buy free-standing plastic picture frames (available in 8″ x 10″ or 5″ x 7″ from discount stores) for each table.

3. Create a different table identifier for each table in the appropriate size and place it in a frame.

4. Place a sign in the middle of each student table.

Sample Room Layout

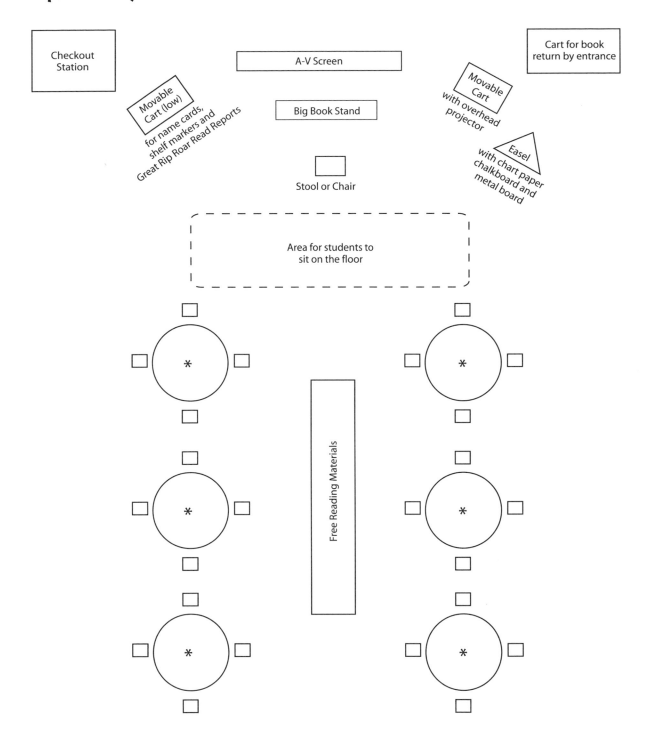

* table signs, baskets with colors, scissors, pencils and glue

One or more of the movable carts and/or big book stand should include storage for lesson materials for current lessons and lesson plan book.

❁ Lesson Learning Ideas ❁

The lesson learning ideas encompass six instructional strands. See page 6 for an explanation of each strand.

Library Skills

- Is familiar with a library setting

- Applies library manners

- Understands library lesson formats

- Can identify the title, author and illustrator

- Can select books based on personal interest

- Comprehends library management skills

- Can follow circulation procedures

- Is able to appropriately attend to various story sharing methods

- Knows the connection between storytelling and books

- Can take proper care of books

- Uses encyclopedias to locate information

- Knows that materials in the library have a specific location and order

- Can identify the spine and spine label of a book

- Can locate a book in the easy fiction section by the author's last name

- Knows the spine label tells where a book is placed on the shelf

Literature Appreciation

- Participates in investigating character analysis

- Has had experience with various literary genres

- Has an understanding of the concept of artist and illustrator

- Has used fiction and nonfiction materials

- Has an initial understanding of the difference between fiction and nonfiction

- Is familiar with the concept of a sequel

- Understands the concept of variation in folktales

- Understands the concept of characters from works of fiction

- Knows the meaning of award-winning literature

Techniques of Learning

- Has established visual literacy skills
- Has experience in critical thinking questioning
- Has the opportunity to work in cooperative groups
- Has experience with compare and contrast questioning
- Understands and participates in brainstorming activities
- Is able to integrate cues from written and visual text
- Uses organizational formats for learning
- Can transfer learning experiences across multiple situations
- Attends to personal and/or team tasks outside of the whole group setting
- Participates in independent reading
- Takes an active role in recomposing visual and written information

Comprehension

- Has extended personal vocabulary
- Has enhanced personal sight word vocabulary
- Has experience in the comprehension strategy of retelling
- Has the opportunity to apply the comprehension strategy of story structure
- Has the opportunity to participate in experiences that support the acquisition of fluency
- Utilizes the comprehension strategy of prediction
- Is able to set a purpose for reading
- Is able to make connections with prior knowledge and experience
- Can recall, summarize and paraphrase what is listened to and viewed
- Is beginning to comprehend basic text structures

Writing Experiences

- Has participated in a variety of age-appropriate writing experiences
- Can create labels, notes and/or captions
- Is able to generate brief descriptions that use sensory details
- Responds to literature in a variety of written formats
- Uses prewriting strategies such as drawings, brainstorming and/or graphic organizers

- Imitates models of good writing

- Is able to transfer ideas into sentences with appropriate support

- Indicates an understanding of story structure necessary for narrative writing

- Participates in narrative writing experiences

- Participates in descriptive writing experiences

- Has experience with examples of narrative writing and its uses

- Has experience with examples of descriptive writing and its uses

Oral Language

- Has taken part in storytelling and read aloud experiences

- Participates in audience participation storytelling

- Is able to listen to and comprehend a variety of oral presentation formats

- Is able to listen to and comprehend a variety of multimedia presentation formats

- Is developing the ability to respond to what is seen and heard

Teddy Bear Time

🐾 Teddy Bear Time • Lesson 1 🐾

Featured Book

Teddybears in Trouble by Susanna Gretz and Alison Sage.
A & C Black, 1990.

Several teddy bear friends run into trouble when their dog doesn't do what he has been told to do. ISBN 0713632925

Lesson Learning Ideas

Library Skills

- Is familiar with a library setting

- Applies library manners

- Understands library lesson formats

- Can identify the title, author and illustrator

- Is able to appropriately attend to various story sharing methods

Literature Appreciation

- Has had experience with various literary genres—picture book

Techniques of Learning

- Has the opportunity to work in cooperative groups

Oral Language

- Has taken part in storytelling and read aloud experiences

- Is developing the ability to respond to what is seen and heard

Materials

- *Teddybears in Trouble* by Susanna Gretz and Alison Sage

- Teddy Bear pictures for tables (pages 20–22)

- Fred picture (page 23)

share with others.

- Teddy Bear picture for rules (page 24)
- crayons for students

Before Class

1. Enlarge one copy of each teddy bear from pages 20–22 to put on student tables. Place them in clear 8″ x 10″ plastic picture frames so they can stand in the middle of the tables. If you like, paste each bear on a piece of construction paper.

2. Determine how many students will be at each table. Make copies of the Teddy Bear pictures for tables so each child has a bear that matches the bear at his or her table.

3. Copy enough Fred pictures to use in the Hide and Seek activity in step three of the lesson plan. Laminate the pictures before using. Hide the Fred pictures around the library (in the picture book section, at the checkout desk, with the free reading materials, etc.).

4. Make one copy of the teddy bear picture from page 24 for each library rule. Write one rule on each bear and display.

5. Make additional copies of the bears from pages 20–22 for the students to color.

Lesson Plan

1. Have the students sit on the floor where the books will be presented. Introduce the Ready Rhyme from page 7 so children will begin to prepare for listening. When the students are settled, read aloud from *Teddybears in Trouble* by Susanna Gretz and Alison Sage. (Anytime a book is read aloud be sure to indicate the title, author and illustrator by pointing to the names and reading them aloud.) Stop when Louise the teddy bear spots Fred the dog on the other side of the library.

2. Move the students to their tables one table at a time. Hand out the Teddy Bear pictures and have the children find the table that matches their bear.

3. When all of the students are seated, tell them they are going to play a game with Fred from the story. Tell the children that Fred is hidden in some very important places in the library. Explain that you will give clues to see if the children can find Fred.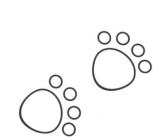

   Clues might include:

   - Fred is hidden behind the librarian. Raise your hand if you know where Fred is.

   - Fred is hidden in the easy book section. Raise your hand if you know where Fred is.

   - Fred is hidden at the computer used for checking out books. Raise your hand if you know where Fred is.

Other items can be added as needed for any given library. In addition, a brief explanation of each person or place Fred highlights can be included.

4. Tell the children that Fred really wants to stay in the library. The teddy bears are going to teach him good library manners so he will be welcomed in a library.

5. Introduce each library rule by reading it aloud and providing an activity to help students remember the rule. Suggestions for rules and activities are:

- Rule: "Do what the librarian asks you to do." Have the children practice this rule by playing The Librarian Says (like Simon Says). Keep the directions simple and praise the students when they follow the directions as stated.

- Rule: "Talk quietly." Explain that teddy bears talk so quietly that you can't even hear them. Demonstrate how people talk in a library and have the children practice by talking quietly to the person next to them. Explain the difference between talking to the group as a whole (like during a story or when playing Find Fred) and when someone is talking to an individual or small group.

- Rule: "Share with others." Demonstrate this rule by giving each child a teddy bear picture to color. Model how one container of colors is shared at a table.

- Rule: "Wait your turn." Demonstrate this rule when it is time to go. Tell the students that one table at a time will be called to line up. For example, ask if all the children at the clown bear table will please line up. Or show the bear pictures one at a time and have the students seated at that table line up.

Teddy Bear Pictures for Tables

Photocopy to desired size.

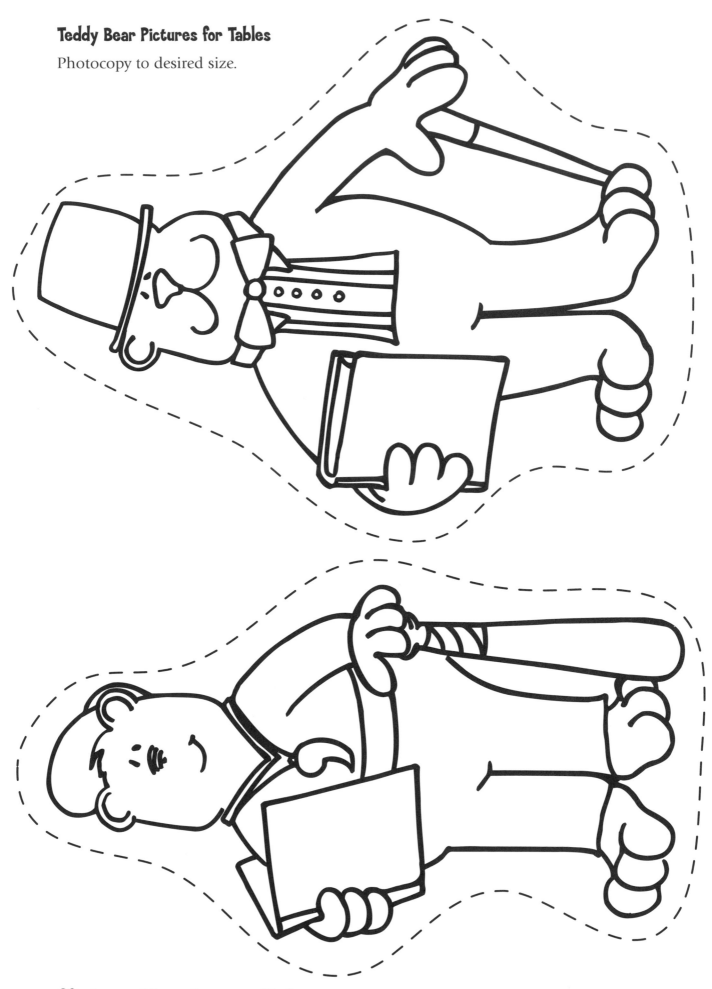

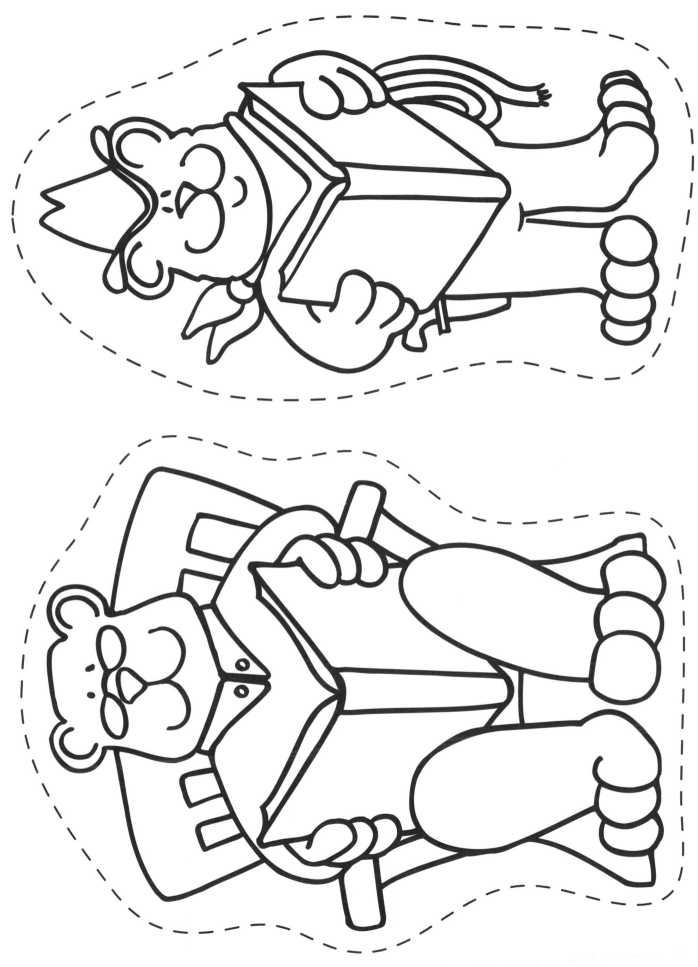

Fred Picture

Photocopy to desired size.

Teddy Bear Picture for Rules

Photocopy to desired size.

🐾 Teddy Bear Time · Lesson 2 🐾

Featured Book

Corduroy by Don Freeman. Viking, 1976.

A toy bear in a department store wants a number of things, but when a little girl finally buys him he finds what he has always wanted most of all.
ISBN 0670241334

Lesson Learning Ideas

Library Skills

- Can identify the title, author and illustrator
- Is able to appropriately attend to various story sharing methods

Literature Appreciation

- Has had experience with various literary genres—picture book

Techniques of Learning

- Has established visual literacy skills
- Has the opportunity to work in cooperative groups
- Is able to integrate cues from written and visual text
- Can transfer learning experiences across multiple situations
- Attends to personal and/or team tasks outside of the whole group setting

Comprehension

- Has experience in the comprehension strategy of retelling

Oral Language

- Has taken part in storytelling and read aloud experiences
- Is able to listen to and comprehend a variety of multimedia presentation formats
- Is developing the ability to respond to what is seen and heard

Materials

- *Corduroy* by Don Freeman, video version (see Ordering Information, page 187)
- *Corduroy* by Don Freeman (paperback) multiple copies or book pictures for display

Before Class

1. Locate enough copies of *Corduroy* so there is one copy for every four students. If enough copies are not available, create picture cards for the book. To do this, cut apart two paperback books and mount each picture from the story on poster board and display.

2. Set the video for start time.

Lesson Plan

1. Show a copy of the book. Read the title and author's name from the cover. Briefly explain the terms "title" and "author."

2. Explain that the book for this week has been made into a video. Show one or two pictures from the book. Tell the children that the teddy bear and the other characters in this video story move.

3. Show the video. Start the video where you see the toy train on the tracks while the credits are rolling. The length of the video is approximately 15 minutes.

4. Move students to their library tables as in lesson 1. Explain that in the library they may sit in a different place each week. This might be different from what they do in their classroom.

5. If time permits, include the visual retelling on page 27 as part of the library lesson. If there is not time, it would be a good way to collaborate with the classroom teacher. Provide all of the materials and the directions for the classroom teacher as a way of showing the library connection to literacy instruction.

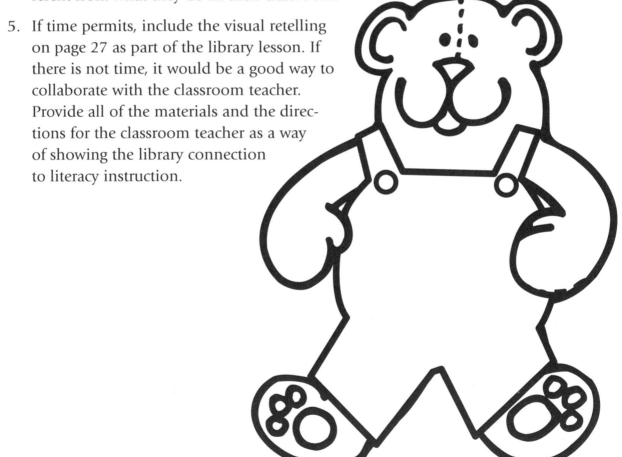

Directions for a Visual Retelling of *Corduroy* by Don Freeman

Start by briefly explaining what a visual retelling is. The best definition for young children might be that they are going to read the pictures. Next, model how to read the pictures. Using the pictures on the first three pages of the book, tell the story segment based on the pictures. Then divide students into groups of four. Provide the materials as suggested on page 25. Select one student to start and have him or her "read the pictures." Rotate the "reading" until each child has spoken within his or her group and the story is complete.

- Student One starts on the page with the little girl walking away with her mother and ends on the page with the second picture of Corduroy on an escalator. (six pages)

- Student Two starts with the page on which Corduroy is in the furniture department and ends on the page where the lamp falls over. (six pages)

- Student Three starts with the page where the night watchman is looking for the source of the noise and ends on the page where Corduroy is asleep on a shelf. (six pages)

- Student Four starts with the little girl looking at Corduroy and goes to the end of the story.

Directions may need to be modified depending on the ability of the students. It is important to allow the students to do as much of the retelling themselves as possible!

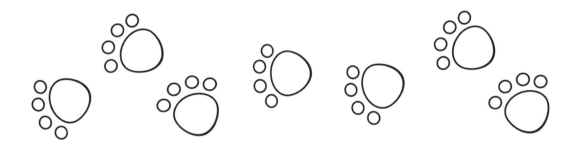

🐾 Teddy Bear Time • Lesson 3 🐾

Featured Book

A Pocket for Corduroy by Don Freeman. Puffin, 1980.

A toy bear who wants a pocket for himself searches for one in a Laundromat. ISBN 0140503528

Lesson Learning Ideas

Library Skills

- Is able to appropriately attend to various story sharing methods

- Can identify the title, author and illustrator

Literature Appreciation

- Has had experiences with various literary genres—picture book

Techniques of Learning

- Has the opportunity to work in cooperative groups

- Understands and participates in brainstorming activities

- Is able to integrate cues from written and visual text

- Uses organizational formats for learning

Comprehension

- Can recall, summarize and paraphrase what is listened to and viewed

- Has extended personal vocabulary

Oral Language

- Has taken part in storytelling and read aloud experiences

- Is able to listen to and comprehend a variety of multimedia presentation formats

- Is developing the ability to respond to what is seen and heard

Materials

- *A Pocket for Corduroy* by Don Freeman book and listening center (see Ordering Information, page 187)

- pictures of Corduroy stamped on index cards (see Ordering Information, page 187)

- graphic organizer "F" (page 31)

- tape recorder and listening center

- stamped pictures of Corduroy

Note: There is a video called *A Pocket for Corduroy* but the plot is very different from the book.

Before Class

1. Prepare one stamped Corduroy picture for each student.

2. Make graphic organizer "F" into a transparency.

Lesson Plan

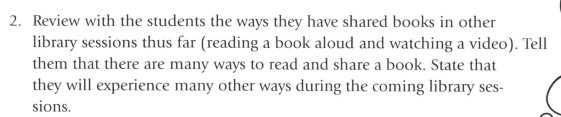

1. Tell the children that they are going to read another story about Corduroy, but this book has been made into a listening center. Someone else is going to read the story to them while they follow along in their books. Demonstrate how headsets are worn when they listen in small groups. For today's story the whole class will listen together without the headsets.

2. Review with the students the ways they have shared books in other library sessions thus far (reading a book aloud and watching a video). Tell them that there are many ways to read and share a book. State that they will experience many other ways during the coming library sessions.

3. Monitor as students listen and follow along to *A Pocket for Corduroy* by Don Freeman.

4. Introduce the word "insisted." Read the sentence in which the word appears. Tell the students that "insisted" means when you are told you have to do something. Ask them who insisted on what in the story. Lisa's mother insisted they leave the Laundromat even though Lisa could not find Corduroy.

5. Use graphic organizer "F." Inform the children that you are going to talk about the facts and feelings surrounding the part in the story where Lisa's mother insisted. Ask the children to list what they remember from that part of the story. As students share their ideas, list them in the top portion of the "F" if they are facts and in the bottom portion if they are feelings.

6. When the students have exhausted their ideas, show them how you categorized them. Ask them how they might feel if someone insisted: a) they leave behind their favorite toy; b) they eat their favorite food; c) they play in the rain; d) they open a gift; e) they go swimming. Note that different items will receive different responses. Help the students notice that every student did not feel the same way about each item. Finally, ask the students to share something they would like to insist upon or not insist upon.

7. Share that in the story Lisa gave Corduroy a card with his name on it to put in his pocket. Give each student a stamped picture of Corduroy as they leave. Tell them that the card has something to do with what they are going to learn in the library the next time.

🐾 Teddy Bear Time • Lesson 4 🐾

Featured Book

Where's My Teddy? by Jez Alborough. Candlewick Press, 1994.

When a small boy named Eddie goes searching for his lost teddy bear in the dark woods, he comes across a gigantic bear with a similar problem. ISBN 1564022803

Lesson Learning Ideas

Library Skills

- Applies library manners

- Can select books based on personal interest

- Can identify the title, author and illustrator

- Can follow circulation procedures

- Is able to appropriately attend to various story sharing methods

Literature Appreciation

- Has had experience with various literary genres—picture book

Techniques of Learning

- Has experience with compare and contrast questioning

- Attends to personal and/or team tasks outside of the whole group setting

- Participates in independent reading

Oral Language

- Is able to listen to and comprehend a variety of oral presentation formats

Materials

- *Where's My Teddy?* by Jez Alborough, big book version and regular sized version (see Ordering Information, page 187)

- miscellaneous picture books for each table of students

- checkout cards for each student

- trays for checkout cards (see Ordering Information, page 187)

Before Class

1. Create a checkout card for each student.

2. Gather enough library books for each table to have two or three per student.

Lesson Plan

1. Share that the next two lessons are stories about a "real" bear and his teddy bear. Today's story is like the Corduroy story because there are lost bears in both stories.

2. Show the regular size copy and the big book version of *Where's My Teddy?* by Jez Alborough. Tell the students that the book has been made very large so a whole group of children can enjoy the story at one time. Read the book aloud.

3. Move the students to their library tables. When all of the students are seated, ask if anyone remembers what they took home with them from the library last time. (A card with a picture of Corduroy on it.)

4. Tell the children that today they are going to get a card like Corduroy did—one with their name on it. Tell them that these cards will stay in the library so that they will be able to check out books.

5. Show the students where their cards will be located. Explain that Corduroy (from the previous session's story) had a pocket for his name card and so does the library. Put out the checkout cards in trays (pockets) and have students practice finding their card. Next class they will check out books to take to their classrooms for the first time. (Students will continue to check out books to go to their classrooms until the end of the Mouse House unit.)

6. Describe how one table at a time will be called to look for their cards.

7. Place a stack of books on each table and explain that they are going to practice finding just the right book for them. Model the procedures for students to select books. Give the students an opportunity to select books to "read" at their tables. Remind them that the boy and the bear in today's story looked for the right teddy bear just like they are looking for the right book.

8. While one or two tables of children locate their cards, the other students can read books at their tables.

🐾 Teddy Bear Time · Lesson 5 🐾

Featured Book

It's the Bear! by Jez Alborough. Candlewick Press, 1996.

Sequel to *Where's My Teddy?* Eddie and his mom go into the woods for a picnic and meet a very large, very hungry bear. ISBN 1564028402

Lesson Learning Ideas

Library Skills

- Can select books based on personal interest

- Can follow circulation procedures

- Is able to appropriately attend to various story sharing methods

- Knows the connection between storytelling and books

Literature Appreciation

- Has had experience with various literary genres—picture book

Techniques of Learning

- Attends to personal and/or team tasks outside of the whole group setting

Oral Language

- Has taken part in storytelling and read aloud experiences

- Is able to listen to and comprehend a variety of multimedia presentation formats

- Is developing the ability to respond to what is seen and heard

Materials

- *It's the Bear!* by Jez Alborough

- LPs for *It's the Bear!* (pages 36–38)

- metal board (see Ordering Information, page 187), magnetic dry erase board, cookie sheet or storytelling apron (see Ordering Information, page 187)

- picnic basket with plastic, color-coded food items or picnic pictures from pages 38–40

- table signs

- copies of the LPs for students to color

- tape recorder and tape of book *(optional)*

Before Class

1. Follow the instructions from page 10 to create the LP presentation visual for *It's the Bear!*

2. Copy enough LPs for each student to have one set to color.

3. Make a tape of the story. *(Optional)*

4. Collect items for real picnic basket or prepare included picnic pictures.

Lesson Plan

1. Tell *It's the Bear!* using the pictures from the LPs. Use a metal board the same way a flannel board would be used, just add the pictures as the story action changes. In order to make the telling easier, tape record someone reading the story onto a cassette. Play the cassette while presenting the LPs. Or tell the story using the LPs and a storytelling apron.

2. Explain to the children that they are ready to start moving to their tables like the older students do. Use the idea of a picnic from the story to introduce the color coding used on the library tables. Have the students face the tables while remaining seated in the listening area. Then bring out a real picnic basket. Take a cloth out of the basket and spread it on the floor. Take food items out of the basket one at a time and ask the students: What color is _____? Items to include might be: corn (yellow), carrot (orange), paper plate (white), carton of chocolate milk (brown), apple (red) or celery (green). After each item's color has been correctly identified, select students to locate the table that has a basket and/or color table sign with the same color.

3. When all of the students are seated, review the book selection and check out procedures. Provide a stack of books at each table for students to select a book to check out to take back to their classroom.*

4. As students finish, allow them to pick up an LP and color it at their table while the rest of the class finishes checking out.

* Kindergarten students will check out books this way for the rest of the year. Students will start taking books home at the end of the Mouse House unit.

Literature Pictures (LPs) for It's the Bear!

Photocopy to desired size.

Teddy Bear Time **37**

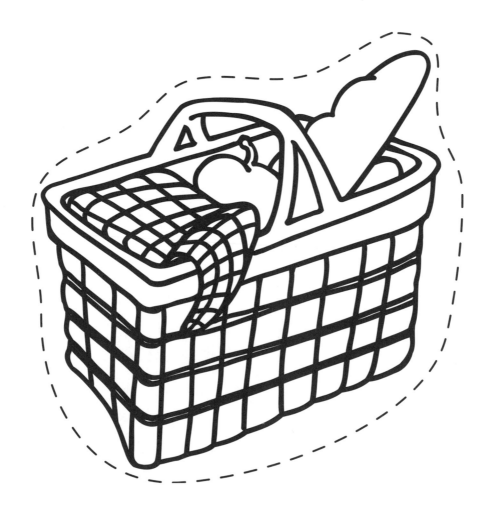

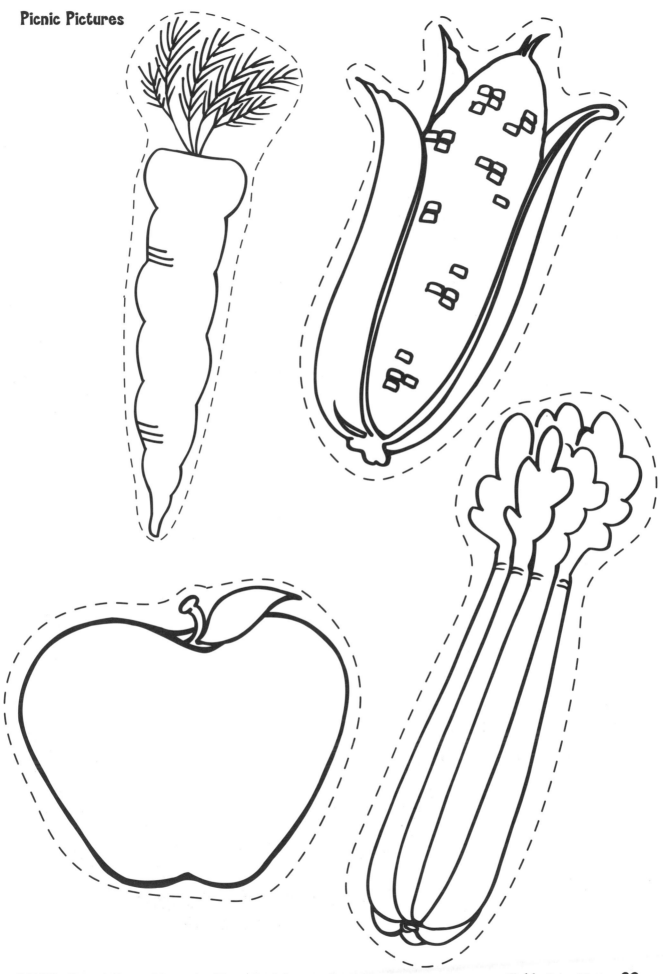

Extra picture

Extra picture

Teddy Bear Time • Lesson 6

Featured Book

Drawing Lessons from a Bear by David McPhail.
Little, Brown and Company, 2000.

A bear explains how he becomes an artist, first experimenting with simple drawings, then continuing to draw things around him and things in his imagination. ISBN 0316563455

Lesson Learning Ideas

Library Skills

- Can identify the title, author and illustrator
- Can select books based on personal interest

Literature Appreciation

- Has an understanding of the concept of artist and illustrator
- Has had experience with various literary genres—picture book

Techniques of Learning

- Has established visual literacy skills
- Understands and participates in brainstorming activities

Comprehension

- Has extended personal vocabulary

Oral Language

- Has taken part in storytelling and read aloud experiences
- Is able to listen and comprehend a variety of oral presentation formats
- Is developing the ability to respond to what is seen and heard

Materials

- *Drawing Lessons from a Bear* by David McPhail
- *Fix-it* by David McPhail *(optional)*
- *The Teddy Bear* by David McPhail *(optional)*

Before Class

Collect all the David McPhail books available in the library collection.

Lesson Plan

1. Display David McPhail's books. Ask the students to look at them and decide on the kinds of animals that appear in each book. If there are not enough books to go around, briefly introduce each book, tell a little about the story and show a few pictures so the children can decide on the animals found in the stories. Make a list of the animals used as characters in David McPhail's books. Count how many of the books include each particular animal.

2. Share with the students all of the available bear books that David McPhail has written (see the list below). Explain that these books were all written by the same author. Show his name on the front of one or two books. Ask the students to find his name on the other books.

3. Tell the students that not only is David McPhail the author, but he also drew the pictures. He likes drawing so much that he combined bears and a book about drawing. Read aloud *Drawing Lessons from a Bear*.

4. Write the words "artist" and "illustrator" on the board or a chart. Ask what it means to be an artist. Then explain that an artist who does the pictures for a book is called an illustrator. Tell the students that when a picture book has only one name on the cover it means that that person drew the pictures **and** wrote the book. As students select books for check out, ask them to figure out if the authors of their books also drew the pictures.

5. If time permits, read another bear book by David McPhail. *Fix-it* or *The Teddy Bear* are good choices for this lesson.

Bear Books by David McPhail:

The Bear's Toothache
Big Brown Bear
Big Brown Bear's Up and Down Day
A Bug, a Bear, and a Boy
A Bug, a Bear, and a Boy Go to School
Emma's Pet
Fix-it
Henry Bear's Christmas
Henry Bear's Park
Jack and Rick
Lost!
Rick is Sick
The Teddy Bear

🐾 Teddy Bear Time • Lesson 7 🐾

Featured Video

The Teddy Bear Factory

Join Freddy Bear and all his friends as they explore a teddy bear factory and learn the history of this cuddly companion in this live-action program that follows production from design to completion.

Lesson Learning Ideas

Library Skills

- Is able to appropriately attend to various story sharing methods

Literature Appreciation

- Has used fiction and nonfiction materials

Techniques of Learning

- Uses organizational formats for learning

- Attends to personal and/or team tasks outside of the whole group setting

Comprehension

- Has experience in the comprehension strategy of retelling

- Can recall, summarize and paraphrase what is listened to and viewed

Oral Language

- Is able to listen and comprehend a variety of multimedia presentation formats

- Is developing the ability to respond to what is seen and heard

Materials

- *The Teddy Bear Factory* video (see Ordering Information, page 187)

- Teddy Bear Factory How-to Book (pages 45–46)

- crayons and scissors

- construction paper and stapler

THIS TEDDY BEAR WAS MADE WITH ♡

Before Class

1. Copy the Teddy Bear Factory How-to Book so each child has one. Precut the pages if necessary.

2. Cue the video to begin right after the narrator bear says, "You see there are hundreds of different kinds of bears."

Lesson Plan:

1. Share with the students that today's lesson is a make-believe field trip to a teddy bear factory. Explain that what they will see is the real way teddy bears are made in some factories and factory stores. Children may be familiar with Build-a-Bear stores that are located in some shopping malls.

2. Show the video. End the video after 13 minutes when the female narrator asks, "Are you ready to make your own teddy bear?" If time permits, play the video to the end of the tape, a total of 16 minutes.

3. Hand out the pages to the teddy bear book. Read aloud the words on each page. Let the children decide the order of the pages. Discuss what happens in each part of the process. Allow the children to draw and color pictures to create a visual instruction book for making a teddy bear. Staple the pages together inside a folded construction paper cover. Allow students to create their own title, author and illustrator information for the cover. Review title, author and illustrator concepts if needed.

Cut out the pieces.

Draw a pattern.

Sew the pieces together.

Stuff the bear.

🐾 Teddy Bear Time · Lesson 8 🐾

Featured Book

The Legend of the Teddy Bear by Frank Murphy. Sleeping Bear Press, 2000.

The origins of America's favorite stuffed animal and how it got its name including the lucky timing of two candy store entrepreneurs.
ISBN 1585360139

Lesson Learning Ideas

Library Skills

• Is able to appropriately attend to various story sharing methods

Literature Appreciation

• Has had experiences with various literary genres—nonfiction

Techniques of Learning

• Has experience in critical thinking questioning

• Has experience with compare and contrast questioning

• Understands and participates in brainstorming activities

• Is able to integrate cues from written and visual text

• Takes an active role in recomposing visual and written information

Comprehension

• Is able to make connections with prior knowledge and experience

Oral Language

• Is able to listen and comprehend a variety of multimedia presentation formats

• Is developing the ability to respond to what is seen and heard

Materials

• *The Legend of the Teddy Bear* by Frank Murphy

• chart tablet or chalkboard and markers

• all the books used in the unit

• paper and crayons

Before Class

Nothing needed.

Lesson Plan

1. Begin by asking students to help you make a list of all the things they know about teddy bears. List the ideas on a chart or board. If the children seem stuck offer leading questions to focus their thinking. Questions might include: What do you know about what teddy bears look like? What do you know about stories about teddy bears?

2. Ask the children what they know about the first teddy bears. If they don't know the legend, help them speculate on what they think might have happened. Remember that it is important for every idea to be included in a brainstorm.

3. Show the cover and read the title of *The Legend of the Teddy Bear*. Briefly explain what a legend is using the information in the Author's Note. If time allows, compare the picture on the cover to the last picture in the book.

4. Read aloud *The Legend of the Teddy Bear*. Brainstorm again about what they know about teddy bears and ask if there is anything else from the book that they would like to add.

5. Using books from the unit, remind the students of all the ways that books have been read or shared. Explain that today is the last day of teddy bear stories. Tell the students what stories they will be doing when they come back to the library next time— Stories in Threes, starting with versions of "The Three Bears."

6. Ask the students to pick one story from the unit that they liked. Have them copy the title of their favorite book onto a small piece of paper. Allow time for the students to draw a cover picture. When all of the pictures are complete, create stacks of pictures for each book title. Have the children count the number in each stack. Use numerals and marks to indicate the number for each title. Assist students in creating a graph about the books. Use a block or student picture to indicate each student who picked each book. If time permits, ask comparison questions pertaining to the graph information.

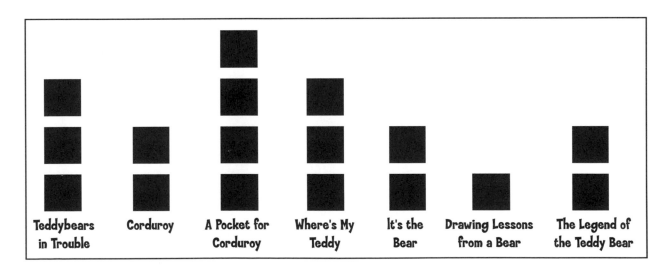

Stories in Threes

Stories in Threes • Lesson 1

Featured Book

Stella Louella's Runaway Book by Lisa Campbell Ernst.
Simon & Schuster, 1998.

As she tries to find the book that she must return to the library, Stella gathers a growing group of people who have all enjoyed the book. ISBN 0689818831

Lesson Learning Ideas

Literature Appreciation

- Has had experiences with various literary genres—folktale
- Understands the concept of variation in folktales

Techniques of Learning

- Has experience in critical thinking questioning
- Understands and participates in brainstorming activities
- Is able to integrate cues from written and visual text

Comprehension

- Utilizes the comprehension strategy of prediction
- Is able to make connections with prior knowledge and experience
- Can recall, summarize and paraphrase what is listened to and viewed

Oral Language

- Is developing the ability to respond to what is seen and heard

Materials

- *Stella Louella's Runaway Book* by Lisa Campbell Ernst
- bag or box to display the books in this unit
- LPs for *Stella Louella's Runaway Book* (pages 54–58)

- metal board

- sentence strips

Before Class

1. Create a container (bag or box) to house all of the books for this unit. Decorate the outside of the container with the number three and/or book-related pictures. If a color copier is available, reduce and copy the covers of all of the books from the unit.

2. Copy the LPs so that each child will have one character to color.

3. Follow the instructions from page 10 to create the LP presentation visual for *Stella Louella's Runaway Book.* Copy the character clues onto separate sentence strips.

Lesson Plan

1. Remind the students that a new series of stories is beginning today. Tell them that the first stories will look and sound very much like the teddy bear stories that they just finished.

2. Ask the students if they can help fill in the title for a story—The Three _____. Have the students share their ideas with a partner. Then ask the class to help make a list. Take all of the answers the children offer. Then explain why there are so many fairy tales and folktales with things in threes in the story. Storytellers use the element of three to keep the audience listening to the story. The idea is that the first time something happens or appears in a story the listener responds, "OK, that's nice." The second time the same type of thing happens the listener responds, "Oh, I remember." And the last time the listener is ready and waiting, "Here it comes, I know it's coming." This is when the teller produces a twist just to keep the listener's attention.

3. Introduce the container holding today's story (and every other story in the unit). Ask the students to look at the container and create some "I wonder" statements about what is going to take place in this unit. Model how this is done by saying "I wonder ..." (add something the box would make you think about). For example, "I wonder if I will hear the story of the three billy goats gruff. I liked that story when I was little."

4. Tell the children that they will hear many stories about threes, including "The Three Bears" and "The Three Pigs." Explain that the stories they will hear will be different ways of telling the familiar stories they know.

5. In today's story there is a book about something with threes but it is hidden in the story. Encourage the students to listen for the clues but to save them until the end of the story.

6. Read aloud or tell *Stella Louella's Runaway Book* using the LP on a metal board. After

reading/telling the story ask if anyone knows the name of Stella Louella's missing library book? Even if a child guesses correctly do not respond. Take all of the guesses and then lead the children through the clues in the book.

7. Play a modified version of Twenty Questions. Line the children up behind you and walk slowly around the library. (This lesson is very heavy on sit and listen/talk activities so the game will help the children get moving.) Give three clues of increasing information about something in the library. Take three guesses with each clue. The student who guesses correctly becomes the head of the line. Do several of these questions before the students return to sitting down. For example:

   • There are many in the library.

   • They come and go in the library.

   • They read books.

   Answer: Children or students

8. Return to the book discussion. Explain that each character in the story offered a clue (in what they said) about the name of Stella Louella's missing book. Match the characters (using the visuals from the LPs) to the clue they offered.

Sam	"I liked the bears"
Mailman	"... especially when they went for a walk"
Tiffany Anne	"I loved the little girl"
Officer Tim	"... classic case of unlawful entry"
Wanda Lynn	"Loved the part about the porridge"
Sal	"... especially when that chair was broken"
Morty	"I loved the part where the little girl tries out the beds!"
mother with baby	"... especially the part about the nap"
Troop of scouts	"... especially when the bears finally returned home"
Duff Morten	"Especially when the bears discovered that girl"
Miss Flynn	"... when the little girl ran through the forest"

Share with the children how the comments each character made fit something about that person. For example: the lady who fixed furniture (Sal) liked the part in the story where the chair was broken. Finally, reveal the name of Stella Louella's book.

9. During free reading time give each child one of the characters from the story to color and keep. Line the children up to go back to their classrooms using the characters they colored. Call them in the order they appeared in the story.

Literature Pictures (LPs) for Stella Louella's Runaway Book

Photocopy to desired size.

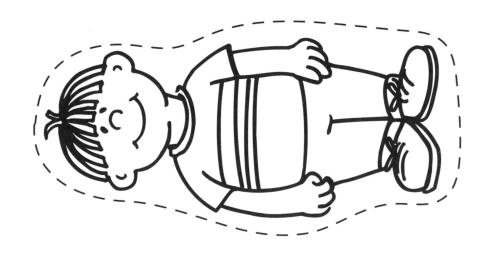

Stories in Threes · Lesson 2

Featured Book

Goldilocks Returns by Lisa Campbell Ernst. Simon & Schuster, 2000.

Fifty years after Goldilocks first met the three bears, she returns to fix up their cottage and soothe her guilty conscience. ISBN 0689825374

Lesson Learning Ideas

Literature Appreciation

- Has had experience with various literary genres—folktales

- Understands the concept of variation in folktales

Techniques of Learning

- Has established visual literacy skills

- Has the opportunity to work in cooperative groups

- Has experience with compare and contrast questioning

- Understands and participates in brainstorming activities

- Attends to personal and/or team tasks outside of the whole group setting

Comprehension

- Utilizes the comprehension strategy of prediction

Materials

- *Goldilocks Returns* by Lisa Campbell Ernst

- *Stella Louella's Runaway Book* by Lisa Campbell Ernst

- *Goldilocks Returns* video (see Ordering Information, page 187)

- *Same-Different Fairy Tales* by Spencer Kagan (see Ordering Information, page 188)

Before Class

Copy, mount and laminate the pictures for the Goldilocks and the Three Bears activity from *Same-Different Fairy Tales*. It is helpful to mount all of the No. 1 pictures on one color of construction paper and all of the No. 2 pictures on a different color.

Lesson Plan

1. Start the lesson by showing the picture of Tiffany Anne sitting on her front steps in *Stella Louella's Runaway Book.* Allow the students to compare this picture to the picture of the young Goldilocks in the beginning of *Goldilocks Returns.* Have the children speculate on how and why this might appear to be the same character.

2. Show the 14½ minute *Goldilocks Returns* video.

3. Divide students into pairs. Give each pair of students the two pictures from the Same-Different activity. Have the children look at the pictures side by side. Explain that there are 20 things that are different in the two pictures. Ask the children to work with a partner to look for differences. After a few minutes, involve the students in creating a class list of the differences. Record the items by number so that the class will know when they found all 20.

4. Explain that there are also 20 things that are alike about the two pictures. Model some examples as this is the harder concept to grasp. Then ask the children to offer a few ideas. Later, during free reading time, allow students to work in pairs or alone with the pictures to locate more of the items that are alike and different.

Stories in Threes • Lesson 3

Featured Book

Deep in the Forest by Brinton Turkle. Puffin, 1992.

A curious bear explores a cabin in the forest, with disastrous results.
ISBN 0140547452

Lesson Learning Ideas

Literature Appreciation

- Understands the concept of variation in folktales

Techniques of Learning

- Has established visual literacy skills
- Understands and participates in brainstorming activities

Comprehension

- Has experience in the comprehension strategy of retelling
- Has the opportunity to apply the comprehension strategy of story structure
- Is able to make connections with prior knowledge and experience
- Can recall, summarize and paraphrase what is listened to and viewed

Writing Experiences

- Has participated in a variety of age-appropriate writing experiences
- Is able to transfer ideas into sentences with appropriate support
- Indicates an understanding of story structure necessary for narrative writing
- Participates in narrative writing experiences

Oral Language

- Is developing the ability to respond to what is seen and heard

Materials:

- *Deep in the Forest* by Brinton Turkle
- sentence strips and markers
- easy release painters' tape

Before Class

Use two copies of the featured book in paperback form to create the writing platform. Cut out the pictures, then mount, number and laminate each illustration from the book. Be sure and include the picture of the bears from the title page.

Lesson Plan

1. Explain to the students that today's story is a wordless book. Show the book and indicate the lack of text. Discuss with the children how someone would "read" this book.

2. Begin the story with the picture of the mother bear and her three cubs on the title page. Start the picture reading by saying: "Once upon a time there was a mother bear who had three baby bear cubs. One day, while the cubs were playing deep in the forest, one of the cubs saw something far off in the distance that he had never seen before. He didn't know it was a log cabin where people lived. He was curious! So he set out on his own to find out what was what."

3. Introduce one picture at a time and have the children locate the bear cub in the picture.

4. When you have gone through the whole story once, go back and start at the beginning. This time have the children tell what they think is happening in the picture. Translate the ideas into sentences written on sentence strips. Reread the sentences that go with each picture as they are created. Attach the sentences to each illustration with painters' tape (this will not damage the pictures). Allow the students to talk all the way through the story. Translating the ideas into sentences would take too long to complete in one kindergarten session. If numerous classes of kindergarten students attend library at one school, the whole story can be written—each class can create a few pages until the story is completed.

🎲 Stories in Threes • Lesson 4 🎲

Featured Book

The Three Pigs **by David Wiesner. Houghton Mifflin, 2001.**

The three pigs escape the wolf by going into another world where they meet the cat and the fiddle, the cow that jumped over the moon and a dragon. ISBN 0618007016

Lesson Learning Ideas

Library Skills

- Can identify the title, author and illustrator

- Knows the connection between storytelling and books

- Uses encyclopedias to locate information

Literature Appreciation

- Has an understanding of the concept of artist and illustrator

- Has had experience with various literary genres—folktales

- Understands the concept of variation in folktales

- Knows the meaning of award-winning literature

Techniques of Learning

- Has established visual literacy skills

- Is able to integrate cues from written and visual text

Comprehension

- Utilizes the comprehension strategy of prediction

Materials

- *The Three Pigs* by David Wiesner (multiple copies if possible)

- library books with Caldecott Medals and Honor seals

- Caldecott Medal information from World Book Encyclopedia

- "Pigs in Space" from *School Library Journal*, November 2001, Vol. 47, issue 11, page 48 *(optional)*

Before Class

1. Read through the information on the Caldecott Medal and be ready to share it in a way the children will understand.

2. Practice reading/telling this book (it is presented in an unusual way). The person sharing the story will need to support student comprehension by telling the pictures as well as reading the words.

3. Read through the information in the *School Library Journal* article and be ready to share the content. *(Optional)*

Lesson Plan

1. Use the computer-based version or the traditional book version of the World Book Encyclopedia for this lesson. Briefly share the uses for encyclopedias. Show the encyclopedia's article, in which an explanation is given for the Caldecott Medal. A good comparison might include asking the children to imagine that they won an award for being the best kindergarten student in their state. Explain that this would be like winning the Caldecott Medal.

2. Show the featured book and share the meaning of the gold medal on the book jacket. Share other books with the silver honor sticker. Explain that the book for today's lesson won the Caldecott Medal in 2002.

3. Direct the children's attention to the cover of the book. Ask the students what they think the story is for today. Ask who drew the pictures for the story. Then explain that this is not the ordinary telling of "The Three Pigs."

4. Read the words and tell the pictures. Provide adequate time for the students to view the pictures on each page. If possible, have student pairs follow along using personal copies of the book.

5. Share some of the information about the book and the author from the *School Library Journal* article. Children may find the cover particularly interesting. Share how David Wiesner made the colors meaningful. Go back to the pictures in the book and examine the pigs more closely. Focus attention on how the pigs' looks change as they fall out of the traditional story and as they enter and exit each story they visit.

6. In the books for students to check out, include other books by David Wiesner as well as other Caldecott Medal and Caldecott Honor books. Allow students time to go on a scavenger hunt at their tables to see if they can find Caldecott Honor books, then Caldecott Medal books. Finally, see if they can find other books by Wiesner. How did they know when they found a book by David Wiesner?

   Note: Numerous book-related activities appear online at *www.vickiblackwell.com/lit/threepigs.html.*

Featured Book

The Three Little Javelinas by Susan Lowell. Rising Moon Books, 1992.
A southwestern adaptation of "The Three Little Pigs." ISBN 0873585429

Lesson Learning Ideas

Literature Appreciation

- Has had experience with various literary genres—folktales

- Understands the concept of variation in folktales

Techniques of Learning

- Has the opportunity to work in cooperative groups

- Has experience with compare and contrast questioning

- Understands and participates in brainstorming activities

- Is able to integrate cues from written and visual text

- Can transfer learning experiences across multiple situations

Materials

- *The Three Little Javelinas* by Susan Lowell

- *Same-Different Fairy Tales* by Spencer Kagan (see Ordering Information, page 188)

- tape and player

- traditional versions of "The Three Pigs" in picture book format

- Same and Different Pigs (page 67)

Before Class

1. Copy, mount and laminate the pictures for the The Three Little Pigs activity from *Same-Different Fairy Tales*. Mount all of the No. 1 pictures on one color construction paper and all of the No. 2 pictures on a different color.

2. Use two copies of *The Three Little Javelinas*. Cut the pictures out and mount them on one side of a piece of poster board. Mount the text that accompanies the illustration on the back of the picture. Number the posters and laminate.

3. Find an older student or adult with a background in Spanish to create a read-along tape of the story.

4. Make a copy of the Same and Different Pigs worksheet for each student.

Lesson Plan

1. Review the directions for participating in the Same-Different activity from Lesson 2. Explain that the students will have an opportunity to do a Three Pigs version at the end of the lesson during free reading time.

2. Remove the poster story and/or book from the container. Introduce the name of the person who made the tape of the story. Play the tape and show the pictures from *The Three Little Javelinas.*

3. Explain that the next activity could be a called a compare and contrast. This is another way of saying same and different. Tell the students that they are going to use the skills they learned about same and different pictures. They are going to create their own version of a compare/contrast based on the story.

4. Share the illustrations from one of the traditional picture book versions of "The Three Pigs" (see the list below). Focus the students' attention on the pigs in both stories. As a class, create a written list of things that are different.

5. Hand out the worksheets. Explain that on the left side the students should draw the way the pigs look in the traditional story. On the right they should draw a picture of a Javelina. Remind students to include as many of the things that make them different as possible.

6. During free reading time, allow students to work with the Kagan Same-Different pictures individually or in pairs. If the students seem to be comfortable with the process, increase the difficulty by having the students only look at one picture. Instruct them to ask questions that begin with "Do you have ..." in order to find the similarities or differences. Each student asks one question at a time. Questioning should shift back and forth between the student partners.

Traditional Versions of "The Three Pigs"

- *The Three Little Pigs* by Paul Galdone
- *The Three Little Pigs* by Margaret Hillert
- *Three Little Pigs* by James Marshall
- *The Three Little Pigs* by Barry Moser
- *The Three Little Pigs* by Patricia Seibert
- *The Three Little Pigs* by Harriet Ziefert

Same and Different Pigs

Traditional Pig	Little Javelina

Stories in Threes • Lesson 6

Featured Book

Wait! No Paint! by Bruce Whatley. HarperCollins, 2001.

The three little pigs are in their usual trouble with the big bad wolf, until a mysterious voice (the illustrator) gets involved and mixes things up.
ISBN 0060282703

Lesson Learning Ideas

Literature Appreciation

- Has an understanding of the concept of artist and illustrator

- Has had experience with various literary genres—folktales

- Understands the concept of variation in folktales

Techniques of Learning

- Has established visual literacy skills

- Has experience in critical thinking questioning

Comprehension

- Has experience in the comprehension strategy of retelling

Oral Language

- Is developing the ability to respond to what is seen and heard

Materials

- Concentration Game—see instructions in Before Class section

- *Wait! No Paint!* by Bruce Whatley

- various picture books of "The Three Little Pigs" (page 66)

- LPs for "The Three Little Pigs" (pages 70–73)

- scissors and crayons

Before Class

1. Create a concentration game.

   - Make two copies (color if possible) of the covers of several books about the three pigs. Make enough pictures so that there are at least five sets of picture pairs. Laminate the pictures.

   - Gather enough file folders to have one for each picture. Number the folders one to ten or higher on the outside of each folder.

   - Laminate the folders, then open them up and cut a small slit near the top of the inside of the folder. Use a paper clip to hold the picture in place. After the lesson save the folders to use in other games of concentration.

2. Make copies of the LPs so that each child will have one character and one house.

Lesson Plan

1. Read aloud *Wait! No Paint!*

2. Remind the students that in the first lesson about the three pigs they met someone who had won awards for the pictures they drew for books. Emphasize that the illustrator is someone who draws the pictures for books. Ask, "What were some of the things the illustrator did in this book?"

3. Play a game of illustrator match. Explain to the students how to play concentration. Tell them they will be trying to match the artwork of book illustrators. Play the game. It can be played several times because the pictures can easily be moved from folder to folder.

4. Break students into groups of four children each. Give one story picture (character and house) to each child and have them color and cut it out.

5. Explain that the children are going to tell/play the traditional version of "The Three Little Pigs." Read or tell the story once with the students moving the story pieces they have created. If possible, let the students do the telling and picture movements a second time.

Literature Pictures (LPs) for The Three Little Pigs

Photocopy to desired size.

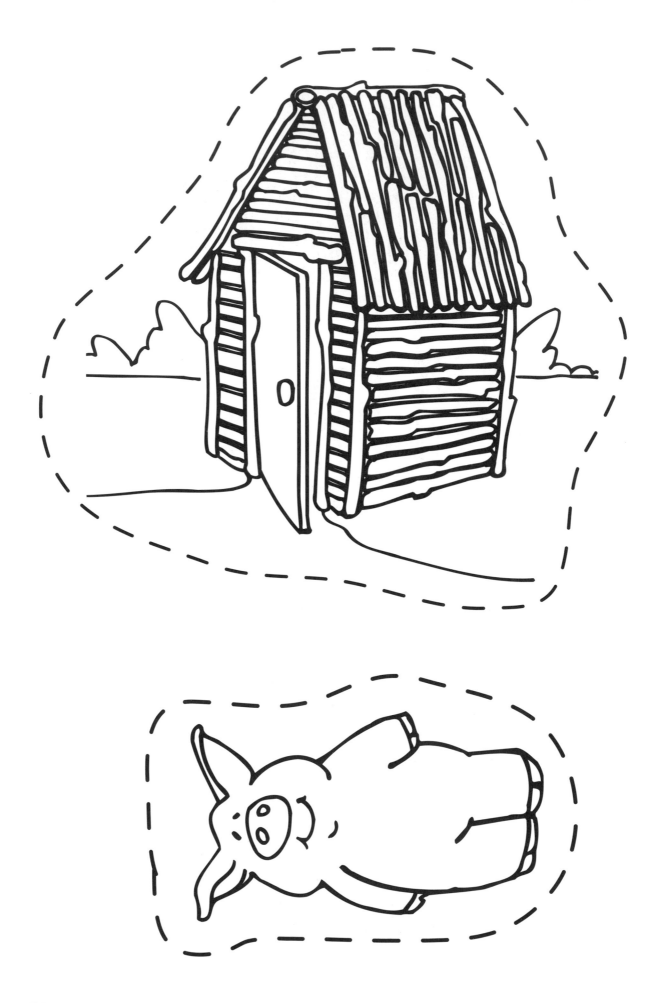

Out Foxed

Out Foxed · Lesson 1

Featured Book

Wings: A Tale of Two Chickens by James Marshall. Houghton Mifflin, 2003.

Harriet the chicken rescues her foolish friend from the clutches of a wily fox. ISBN 0618225870

Lesson Learning Ideas

Literature Appreciation

- Participates in investigating character analysis

Techniques of Learning

- Understands and participates in brainstorming activities

- Has experience in critical thinking questioning

Comprehension

- Has extended personal vocabulary

- Utilizes the comprehension strategy of prediction

- Can recall, summarize and paraphrase what is listened to and viewed

Oral Language

- Is able to listen to and comprehend a variety of multimedia presentation formats

Materials

- *Wings: A Tale of Two Chickens* by James Marshall, video version (see Ordering Information, page 188)

- coloring sheet (page 79)

- copies of all books from unit

- crayons

Before Class

Make copies of page 79 for each student.

Lesson Plan

1. Tell the children that today they are going to see a video of *Wings: A Tale of Two Chickens* (eight minutes). Ask the students to watch the story to see if they can guess why it is being shown as part of a library class.

2. After the video, have the children share their ideas. Explain that a unit is a group (series) of lessons about the same thing (topic). Show the covers of the books that will be covered in this unit. Read the titles and see if the students can decide what the topic is for this unit. Tell them the unit is called Out Foxed because there is an old saying that when you're tricked you are outfoxed.

3. Tell the students that there is another old saying about foxes that refers to someone being as "sly as a fox." Define "sly" as someone who plays tricks on others to get the better of them and/or someone who gets into trouble by pretending to be something he or she is not.

4. Take the children through the book and find things Mr. Johnson did to prove that he was sly. Examples include: getting Winnie to go with him in a balloon, getting Winnie to eat raspberry tarts to fatten her up, putting on a chicken costume, getting Winnie to go into the bag for sardines and saying he had laundry in his bag when asked. Ask the children: What did Harriet do that outfoxed Mr. Johnson?

5. Present one or more of the following questions one at a time for student consideration. Allow children to discuss ideas with a partner before opening up the discussion to the whole class.

   Question A: Which character are you most like—Harriet, Winnie or Mr. Johnson? Why?

   Question B: Why would you want to be friends with Winnie? (Harriet) (Mr. Johnson)

   Question C: Describe Harriet. (Winnie) (Mr. Johnson)

6. Give each student a picture from the story to color and take home.

Today we read
Wings: A Tale of Two Chickens
by James Marshall.

Ask me why it is important to read.

Out Foxed · Lesson 2

Featured Book

Rosie's Walk by Pat Hutchins. Simon & Schuster, 1968.

Although unaware that a fox is after her as she takes a walk around the farm-yard, Rosie the hen still manages to lead him into one accident after another. ISBN 0027458504

Lesson Learning Ideas

Library Skills

- Can identify the title, author and illustrator

Literature Appreciation

- Has an understanding of the concept of artist and illustrator

Techniques of Learning

- Has established visual literacy skills

- Is able to integrate cues from written and visual text

Comprehension

- Utilizes the comprehension strategy of prediction

- Has enhanced personal sight word vocabulary

Writing Experiences

- Has participated in a variety of age-appropriate writing experiences

- Uses prewriting strategies such as drawings, brain-storming and/or graphic organizers

Materials

- *Rosie's Walk* by Pat Hutchins, big book version (see Ordering Information, page 188)

- stamps of Rosie and the fox (see Ordering Information, page 188)

- stamp pads

- self-adhesive name tag labels

- classroom book of *Rosie's Walk* (pages 82–87)

- crayons

- construction paper

- stapler

Before Class

1. Copy the pages for the classroom book of *Rosie's Walk*.

2. Use stamps to create one picture of Rosie and one of the fox on name tag labels for each child.

Lesson Plan

1. Begin by reading aloud *Rosie's Walk*. Point to the words as you read them. Pause at the end of the text on the first page. Ask the students to look at the pictures and tell what else is going on in addition to Rosie going for a walk. Give the children time to share, then explain that this is a true picture book. A picture book is one in which at least half of the story is told in the pictures. Advise the children to watch the pictures carefully to get the whole story.

2. Finish reading the book, then turn back to the front cover. Read the title and author again. Ask who created the pictures. Ask the students to explain how they knew the answer.

3. Share with the children that they are going to have a chance to be the illustrator for this story. Before students start to work provide examples in which students followed the instructions correctly and some where they did not. Use these examples in a discussion with the students before they start to work on their own pictures.

4. Give each student one of the pages from the story and two labels with a picture of Rosie on one and a picture of the fox on the other. Have the students draw everything in the picture except Rosie and the fox. When they complete their pictures, help them peel the backing off the labels and place them on their picture. When the students complete this activity they can put their pictures together to make "picture books" of the story. Let each group of students create a book cover that includes the names of all of the illustrators.

5. Place the completed books in the free reading area for students to enjoy when they come to the library.

Rosie the hen went for a walk ... across the yard

around the pond

over the haystack

past the mill

through the fence

under the beehives.

Out Foxed · Lesson 3

Featured Book

Fox Tale Soup **by Tony Bonning. Simon & Schuster, 2001.**

In this version of the familiar tale, a hungry fox tricks some barnyard animals into contributing the necessary ingredients for making his delicious stone soup. ISBN 0689849001

Lesson Learning Ideas

Literature Appreciation

- Has had experience with various literary genres—folktale

- Understands the concept of variation in folktales

Techniques of Learning

- Has the opportunity to work in cooperative groups

- Has experience with compare and contrast questioning

- Is able to integrate cues from written and visual text

- Can transfer learning experiences across multiple situations

- Attends to personal and/or team tasks outside of the whole group setting

Comprehension

- Has experience in the comprehension strategy of retelling

- Has the opportunity to apply the comprehension strategy of story structure

- Has the opportunity to participate in experiences that support the acquisition of fluency

- Can recall, summarize and paraphrase what is listened to and viewed

Oral Language

- Has taken part in storytelling and read aloud experiences

- Participates in audience participation storytelling

- Is developing the ability to respond to what is seen and heard

Materials

- *Fox Tale Soup* by Tony Bonning
- plastic container that looks like a cook pot
- large rock and a bucket
- salt and pepper shakers and a cooking spoon
- plastic vegetables: turnip, carrot, cabbage, corn
- other versions of the story "Stone Soup" (see the list below)
- art supplies *(optional)*

Before Class

1. Practice telling the story using the objects listed above.
2. Gather as many versions of "Stone Soup" as possible.

Lesson Plan

1. Use the objects in the materials list to tell/read *Fox Tale Soup*. Allow several students to play the part of the animals. When the story indicates a certain animal provided something for the soup let that child/animal character bring that item to the pot.

2. When the story is over, ask the students to turn to a partner and tell how the fox was sly. Give the students time to share, then ask for several students to share with the entire group.

3. Remind students of the concept of a folktale. A folktale is a story where the original teller is unknown. Folktales were handed down from one teller to the next, often with changes made with each retelling. In folklore the same story often appears in various locations. Ask the students if they can think of some folktales presented in the library earlier in the year.

4. Provide small groups of students with one of the versions of "Stone Soup" from the list below.

5. Briefly introduce each book to the class. Allow time for each group to read the pictures in their book. Provide an opportunity for the groups to compare their books to the featured book. For example, students could work together within their groups to draw pictures of all of the characters in their book. As a whole class the pictures could be used to decide which characters were found most often in the stories or who was the main character in each story.

   Bone Button Borscht by Aubrey Davis. Kids Can Press, 1997. Poverty has made the people of a small town stingy and sour, but the arrival of an old beggar who claims he can make borscht from buttons teaches them the value of friendship and sharing.

Button Soup by Doris Orgel. Bantam Books, 1994. In this modern version of the French folktale "Stone Soup," Rag-Tag Meg shows the neighborhood how to make a delicious pot of soup starting with only water and an old wooden button.

Stone Soup retold by Heather Forest. August House, 2000. Two hungry travelers use a stone as a soup starter and demonstrate the benefits of sharing. Includes a recipe for soup.

Stone Soup by Ann McGovern. Scholastic, 1986. When a little old lady claims she has no food to give him, a hungry young man proceeds to make soup with a stone and water.

Stone Soup by Jon Muth. Scholastic, 2003. Three hungry Chinese monks charm a poor village into making enough soup to feed them all.

Stone Soup by Tony Ross. Puffin, 1991. A clever hen manages to stall a hungry wolf's plans to make a meal of her by persuading him to taste her stone soup first.

Stone Soup: An Old Tale by Marcia Brown. Simon & Schuster, 1991. When three hungry soldiers come to town where all the food has been hidden, they set out to make soup of water and stones, and all the town enjoys a feast.

Tumbleweed Stew by Susan Stevens Crummel. Harcourt, 2003. Jack Rabbit tricks the other animals into helping him make a pot of tumbleweed stew.

Out Foxed · Lesson 4

Featured Books

Fox Tale Soup by Tony Bonning. Simon & Schuster, 2001.

In this version of the familiar tale, a hungry fox tricks some barnyard animals into contributing the necessary ingredients for making his delicious stone soup. ISBN 0689849001

The Tale of Tricky Fox: A New England Trickster Tale retold by Jim Aylesworth. Scholastic, 2001.

Tricky Fox uses his sack to trick everyone he meets into giving him ever more valuable items. ISBN 0439095433

Lesson Learning Ideas

Literature Appreciation

- Has had experience with various literary genres—folktale
- Understands the concept of variation in folktales

Techniques of Learning

- Has experience with compare and contrast questioning
- Is able to integrate cues from written and visual text
- Uses organizational formats for learning
- Can transfer learning experiences across multiple situations
- Attends to personal and/or team tasks outside of the whole group setting

Comprehension

- Has experience in the comprehension strategy of retelling
- Has the opportunity to apply the comprehension strategy of story structure
- Has the opportunity to participate in experiences that support the acquisition of fluency
- Can recall, summarize and paraphrase what is listened to and viewed

Oral Language

- Has taken part in storytelling and read aloud experiences
- Is able to listen to and comprehend a variety of multimedia presentation formats

Materials

- *Fox Tale Soup* by Tony Bonning
- *The Tale of Tricky Fox* retold by Jim Aylesworth, video version (see Ordering Information, page 188)
- LPs of *The Tale of Tricky Fox* (pages 95–97)
- multiple metal boards, small magnetic boards or metal cookie sheets (see Ordering Information, page 189)
- Plot Sequences for *Fox Tale Soup* (page 93–94)
- Graphic Organizer Comparison Charts (pages 98–99)
- chart tablet and markers or chalkboard

Before Class

1. Create multiple copies of the metal board story of *The Tale of Tricky Fox*. Follow the instructions from page 10 to create the LPs presentation visuals.

2. Make the plot sequence chart and graphic organizer into transparencies.

Lesson Plan

1. Remind students of the versions of the "Stone Soup" folktale they heard in the last lesson. Inform them that it will take two lessons to complete the next comparison of folktales about foxes.

2. Question the students about the plot sequences from *Fox Tale Soup*. Write down the students' ideas as they list the different things that took place in order to create the soup. For instance, water was asked for. Use the pictures from the book to help if needed. Using the chart on page 93, have the children rearrange the items so that they are in sequential order. Explain that you want them to do the same thing after they listen to today's story.

3. Show eight-minute video of *The Tale of Tricky Fox*.

4. Give each group of two to four students a copy of the LP pieces for this story. Allow them time to work in their groups to put the objects in order as they happened in the story.

5. As a whole group, introduce the concept of problem and plot as part of story structure. Discuss how the use of story structure components will help the students comprehend the stories they read. Ask what the fox's problem was in *Fox Tale Soup*. Then explain that the fox in this story had the same problem but he tried to fix it in a slightly different way.

6. Use the graphic organizer with the children to lay out the story problem and the plot sequences for this story. Save the information for the next lesson.

Plot Sequences for
Fox Tale Soup

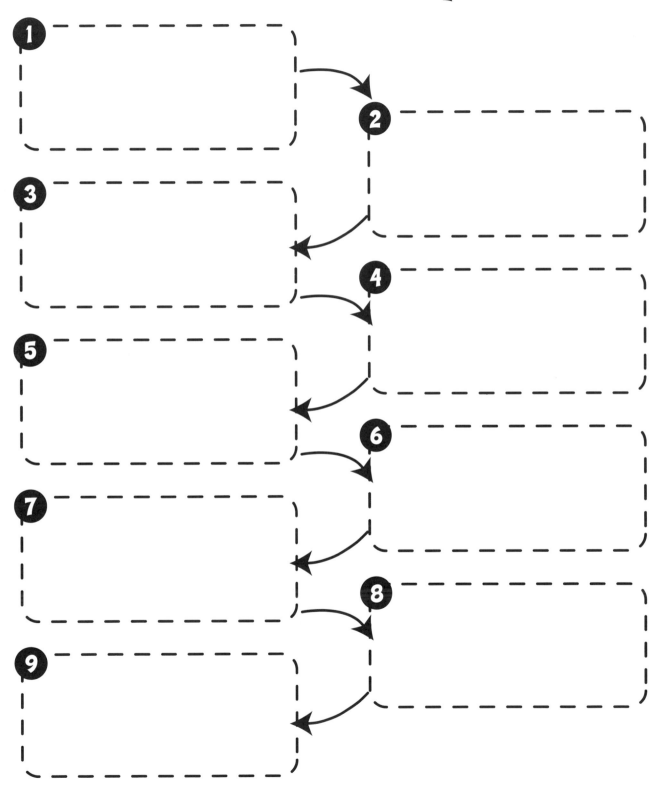

Plot Sequences for Fox Tale Soup Answer Key

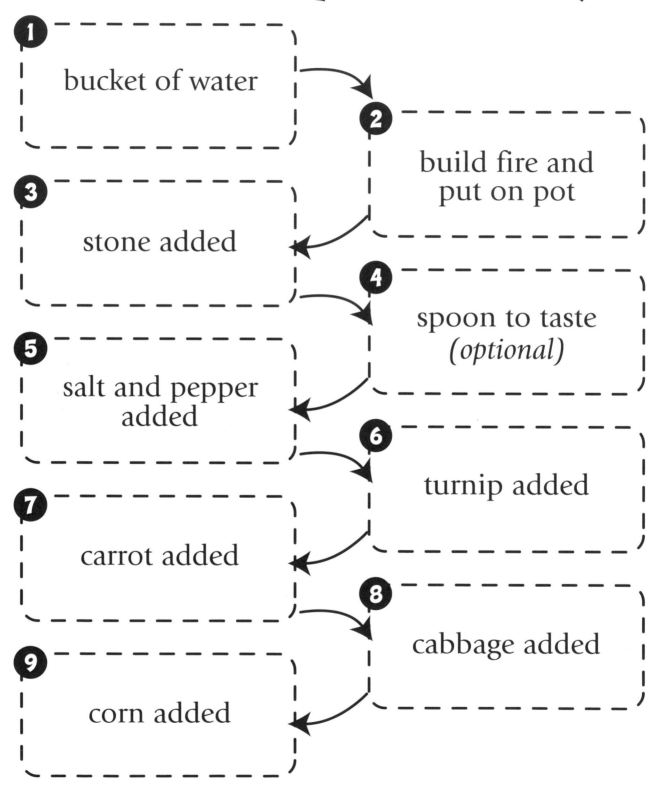

1 bucket of water

2 build fire and put on pot

3 stone added

4 spoon to taste *(optional)*

5 salt and pepper added

6 turnip added

7 carrot added

8 cabbage added

9 corn added

Literature Pictures (LPs) for The Tale of the Tricky Fox

Photocopy to desired size.

The Tale of the Tricky Fox
Graphic Organizer Comparison Chart

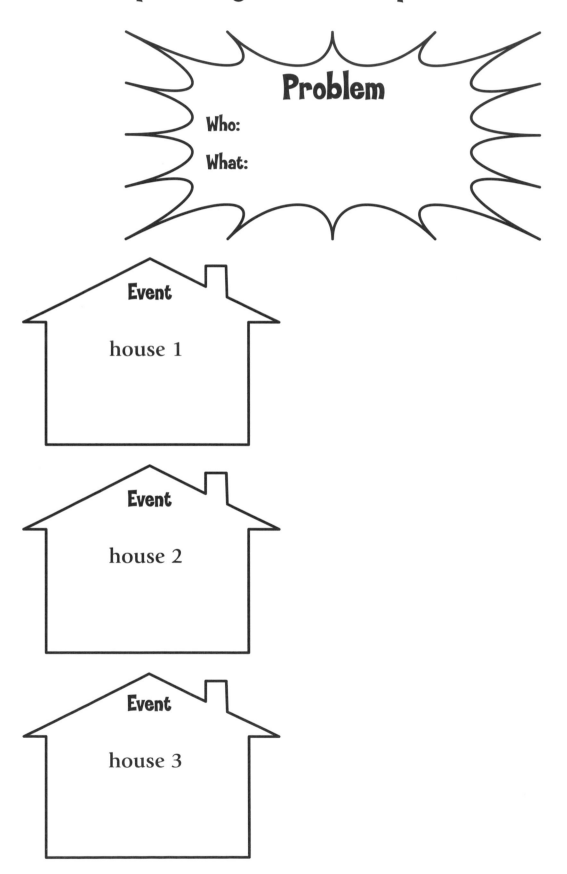

Problem

Who:

What:

Event

house 1

Event

house 2

Event

house 3

The Tale of the Tricky Fox
Graphic Organizer Comparison Chart

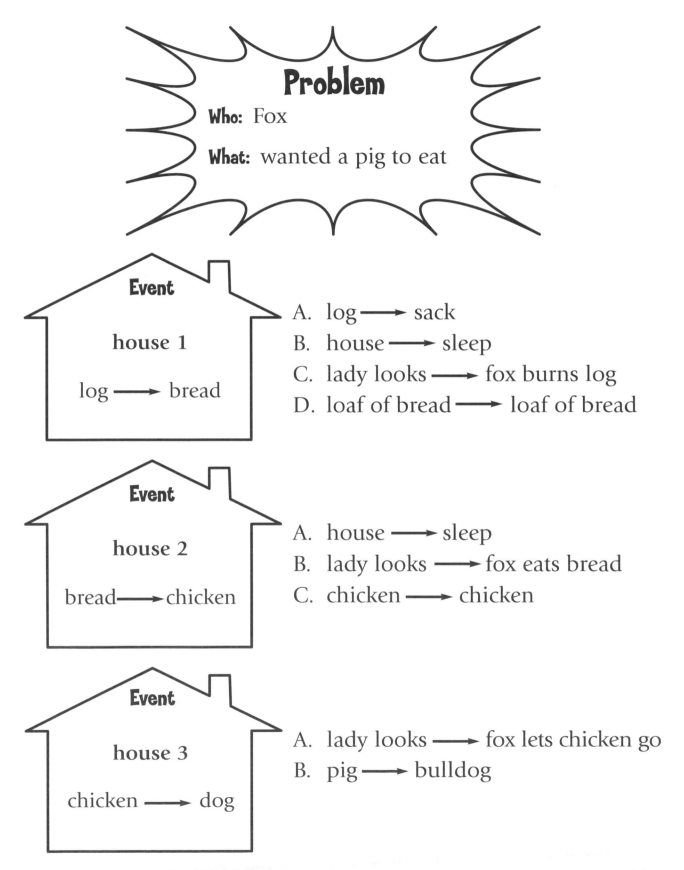

Problem

Who: Fox

What: wanted a pig to eat

Event

house 1

log ⟶ bread

A. log ⟶ sack
B. house ⟶ sleep
C. lady looks ⟶ fox burns log
D. loaf of bread ⟶ loaf of bread

Event

house 2

bread ⟶ chicken

A. house ⟶ sleep
B. lady looks ⟶ fox eats bread
C. chicken ⟶ chicken

Event

house 3

chicken ⟶ dog

A. lady looks ⟶ fox lets chicken go
B. pig ⟶ bulldog

Out Foxed · Lesson 5

Featured Book

What's in Fox's Sack? by Paul Galdone. Houghton Mifflin, 1982.

When a woman lets out the bumblebee that he put in his sack, a wily fox replaces it with a rooster, a pig and finally a little boy, which leads to his downfall. ISBN 0899190626

Lesson Learning Ideas

Literature Appreciation

- Has had experience with various literary genres—folktale

- Understands the concept of variation in folktales

Techniques of Learning

- Has established visual literacy skills

- Has the opportunity to work in cooperative groups

- Has experience with compare and contrast questioning

- Is able to integrate cues from written and visual text

- Uses organizational formats for learning

- Can transfer learning experiences across multiple situations

- Attends to personal and/or team tasks outside of the whole group setting

Comprehension

- Has experience in the comprehension strategy of retelling

- Has the opportunity to apply the comprehension strategy of story structure

- Has the opportunity to participate in experiences that support the acquisition of fluency

- Can recall, summarize and paraphrase what is listened to and viewed

Oral Language

- Has taken part in storytelling and read aloud experiences

- Is developing the ability to respond to what is seen and heard

Materials

- *What's in Fox's Sack?* by Paul Galdone

- LPs of *What's in Fox's Sack?* (pages 104–105)

- metal board, magnetic white board, cookie sheet or Velcro apron (see Ordering Information, page 189)

- graphic organizer and information from lesson 4 along with graphic organizer for current lesson (see pages 102–103)

Before Class

1. Practice telling/reading the story. You may want to add a short refrain to the story right before the lady opens the sack each time. Use the tune from "Who Wrote the Book of Love" but change the words to "I wonder, wonder, wonder, wonder, what! What's in the fox's sack?"

2. Make a presentation copy of the LP pieces for *What's in Fox's Sack?* In addition, make multiple sets for the students to use. Students can do the coloring for the multiple sets. Follow the instructions from page 10 to create the LP presentation visuals.

3. Make the graphic organizer into a transparency.

Lesson Plan

1. Teach the students the refrain song and ask them to help with it throughout the story. Tell/read *What's in Fox's Sack?* Use the LP pieces on a metal board or Velcro apron to enhance the story and to demonstrate how the LPs can be used for free reading.

2. Using the chart on page 102, lay out the story problem and events for this story. The problem may present difficulty for students. If help is needed ask why the fox would put the bee in his sack.

3. Place the graphic organizer from lesson 4 next to the one for this lesson. Allow the children to compare the two stories while highlighting how the graphic organizers help accomplish the comparison.

4. Divide the students into pairs. Give each pair of students a set of LPs for *What's in Fox's Sack?* or *The Tale of Tricky Fox.* Instruct student pairs to let one student tell the story. The other student places the pieces on a metal board. When both students have had an opportunity to do both jobs, explain how they can use the LPs during free reading time in the library.

What's in Fox's Sack?
Graphic Organizer Comparison Chart

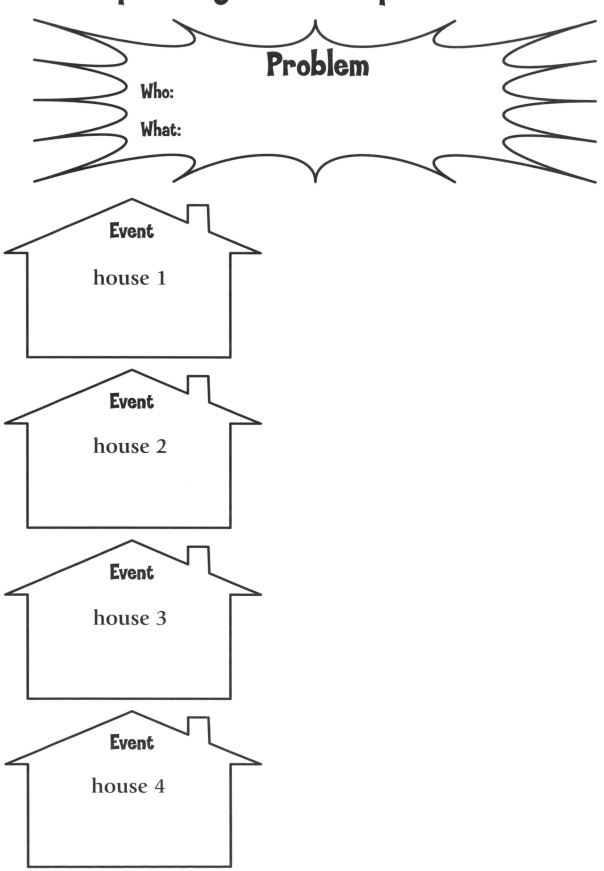

Problem

Who:

What:

Event

house 1

Event

house 2

Event

house 3

Event

house 4

What's in Fox's Sack?
Graphic Organizer Comparison Chart

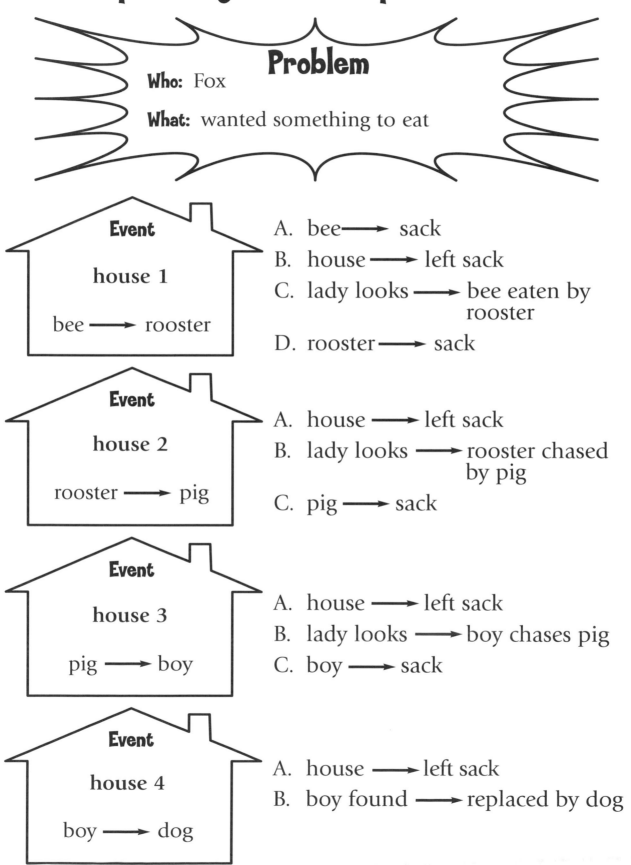

Problem

Who: Fox

What: wanted something to eat

Event

house 1

bee ⟶ rooster

A. bee ⟶ sack
B. house ⟶ left sack
C. lady looks ⟶ bee eaten by rooster
D. rooster ⟶ sack

Event

house 2

rooster ⟶ pig

A. house ⟶ left sack
B. lady looks ⟶ rooster chased by pig
C. pig ⟶ sack

Event

house 3

pig ⟶ boy

A. house ⟶ left sack
B. lady looks ⟶ boy chases pig
C. boy ⟶ sack

Event

house 4

boy ⟶ dog

A. house ⟶ left sack
B. boy found ⟶ replaced by dog

Literature Pictures (LPs) for What's in Fox's Sack?

Photocopy to desired size.

Out Foxed · Lesson 6

Featured Book

Hattie and the Fox by Mem Fox. Simon & Schuster, 1987.

Hattie, a big black hen, discovers a fox in the bushes, which creates various reactions in the other barnyard animals. ISBN 0027354709

Lesson Learning Ideas

Techniques of Learning

- Attends to personal and/or team tasks outside of the whole group setting

- Has experience in critical thinking questioning

Comprehension

- Has the opportunity to participate in experiences that support the acquisition of fluency

- Has experience in the comprehension strategy of retelling

Oral Language

- Has taken part in storytelling and read aloud experiences

- Participates in audience participation storytelling

Materials

- *Hattie and the Fox* by Mem Fox

- one set of the LPs made into puppets (page 108–109)

- picture of the fox (page 75)

Before Class

1. Enlarge the LPs so that they are each 8½" x 11". Mount the pictures on poster board and color them. Write the words the animals say in large letters on the back and front of each picture. Laminate the pictures. To make puppets, glue a craft stick to the back of each picture.

2. Reproduce the picture of the fox. Paste the picture on poster board and laminate to use with the Twenty Questions game.

Lesson Plan

1. Select five students to stand in front of the class. Each will hold a puppet for one of the animals in the story. Divide the rest of the students into five groups. One puppet holder will lead each group. Go over the words each animal says with the children. Explain that when the reader/teller comes to their animal in the story, the group, led by the puppet holder, will say the words the animal says.

2. Tell/read *Hattie and the Fox.*

3. Explain that this is the last lesson in the fox stories unit. Review the meaning of the term "unit." Remind students how LPs and free reading books can be used. Provide ample time for students to use the LPs and free reading materials independently.

4. Introduce the children to the traditional version of Twenty Questions by showing the students a possible hiding place for the fox picture and, as a class, creating some questions that could be asked to help locate the hiding place. Once students begin to grasp how to create questions, send four or five students out of the room. Hide the fox. When the students return they can each ask one question in an effort to try to locate the sly fox.

Literature Pictures (LPs) for Hattie and the Fox

Photocopy to desired size.

Mouse House

Lesson Learning Ideas

Library Skills

- Comprehends library management skills
- Can follow circulation procedures
- Can take proper care of books

Literature Appreciation

- Participates in investigating character analysis
- Understands the concept of characters from works of fiction

Techniques of Learning

- Has experience in critical thinking questioning
- Understands and participates in brainstorming activities
- Is able to integrate cues from written and visual text
- Attends to personal and/or team tasks outside the whole group setting

Comprehension

- Has extended personal vocabulary
- Utilizes the comprehension strategy of prediction
- Is able to set a purpose for reading
- Can recall, summarize and paraphrase what is listened to and viewed

Writing Experiences

- Has experience with examples of narrative writing and its uses

Materials

- *The Character in the Book* by Kaethe Zemach
- *Mouse in the House* by Patricia Baehr
- LPs (pages 116–118)
- chart tablet or chalkboard and markers
- drawing paper
- crayons
- letter to parents (page 119)

Before Class

1. Practice telling the story from *Mouse in the House.*

2. Make copies of the parent letter to send home.

3. Give a copy of the parent letter to the principal.

4. Follow the instructions from page 10 to create the LP visual for *Mouse in the House.*

5. Create a list of mouse books from your collection and make copies to send home.

Lesson Plan

1. Tell the students that today's lesson marks the beginning of a unit about mice. It will help them get ready to check out books to take home for the first time. Introduce and read aloud *The Character in the Book.*

2. Explain that the people or animals in a story (the "who" in a story) are called the characters.

3. Show the cover of *Mouse in the House.* Read the title, author and illustrator. Ask the students who they think are the characters in this story. Tell them that they will revisit the list after they have heard the story.

4. Tell *Mouse in the House.* Use the LPs to enhance the presentation.

5. Return to the discussion of the characters in the story. Have the students extend their story list to include all of the characters. Characters from the book include: Mrs. Teapot, mouse, mailman, baker, cat, butcher, dog, grocer, owl, pet store owner, snake, hardware store owner.

6. Ask the students why Mrs. Teapot and the mouse are the only characters shown on the book cover. Introduce the concept of main characters.

7. Ask the children to name something in the story that is not a character. Give an example, such as "a book," to get them started. Add the student suggestions to the story list.

8. Prompt the children to draw a picture of one of the things on the story list. When the pictures are finished, lead the students in classifying each picture as a character or not a character.

9. Send the letter to parents home with each student and include a list of mouse books from your collection. Read the letter aloud so the children know what they are delivering.

Literature Pictures (LPs) for Mouse in the House

Photocopy to desired size.

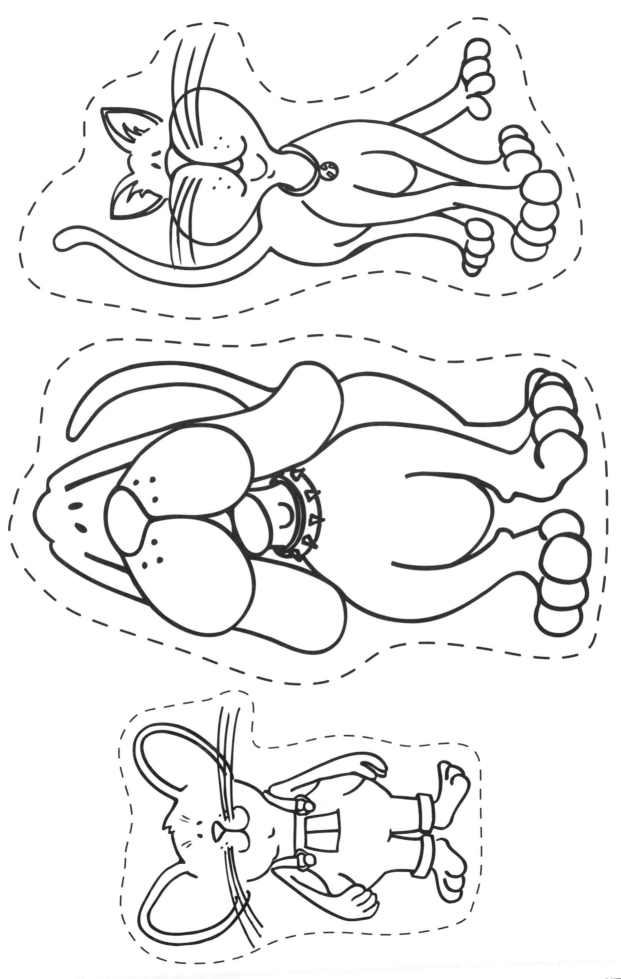

Dear Parents,

This is the beginning of something special for your child! Today we started a unit in the library that will lead to your child checking out books to bring home for the first time. In each class, for the next four class sessions, we will be doing an activity in the library to prepare your child for this important event. Please ask your child to tell you about what we did during library time. The week of _____ will be the first time your child will bring home a library book. It is my hope that you will share this great adventure with your child.

Sincerely,

Featured Book

The Plane by Monique Félix. Harcourt, 1993.

A mouse has an adventure with a plane. ISBN 0152009639

Lesson Learning Ideas

Library Skills

- Can follow circulation procedures

- Knows the connection between storytelling and books

- Can take proper care of books

Techniques of Learning

- Has established visual literacy skills

- Has experience in critical thinking questioning

- Understands and participates in brainstorming activities

- Uses organizational formats for learning

Comprehension

- Has extended personal vocabulary

- Is able to make connections with prior knowledge and experience

Writing Experiences

- Has experience with examples of narrative writing and its uses

Materials

- *The Plane* by Monique Felix

- letter to parents (page 122)

- other books by Monique Felix *(optional)*

- chart

- markers and crayons

- mouse house picture (page 121)

Before Class

1. "Read" the pictures to prepare for the telling of the story.

2. Copy the letters to go home and mouse picture for each student. Give a copy of the parent letter to the principal.

Lesson Plan

1. Share several pages from *The Plane*. Ask if any of the students remember what a book without words is called. Direct the students to the fact that you will be "reading" the pictures to tell the story. Then read/tell the story as you see it.

2. Provide other books by the same author for the children to enjoy (all of them are wordless books). Other titles include: *The Boat, The Colors, The Opposites, The House, The Numbers, The Wind* and *The Alphabet*.

3. Ask the students to help list places animals and people live. You may need to offer suggestions to expand students' thinking. Possibilities include: dog house, barn, tent, trailer and/or cabin. Help the students categorize the list into places for people only, places for animals only and places that can be shared by people and animals.

4. Advise the students that, like the mouse in the story, library books need a home—a place to live. Explain how they should find a special place for their library book away from little people and where they can find it when it is time to return it. Share the parent letter and mouse house picture with the children so they know what to do when they get home.

Dear Parents,

Today in the library we learned about looking for a "home" for your child's library book. This is one of the hardest things for a young child—trying to keep up with a library book that must be returned in

_____.

Help your child designate a permanent place in your home where he or she can always put his or her books when they are not being read. This way we are helping your child build personal responsibility skills which will be useful throughout the rest of his or her life. In addition, this will support the checking out and returning of books as a pleasant, manageable experience even for a five-year-old.

Sincerely,

Mouse House · Lesson 3

Featured Book

If You Give a Mouse a Cookie by Laura Joffe Numeroff. HarperCollins, 1985.

A young boy, having given a cookie to a bossy mouse, is run ragged by the energetic rodent's subsequent requests. ISBN 0060245875

Lesson Learning Ideas

Library Skills

- Can follow circulation procedures

- Knows the connection between storytelling and books

- Can take proper care of books

Techniques of Learning

- Understands and participates in brainstorming activities

- Can transfer learning experiences across multiple situations

Comprehension

- Is able to make connections with prior knowledge and experience

Writing Experience

- Has experience with examples of narrative writing and its uses

Oral Language

- Participates in audience participation storytelling

Materials

- *If You Give a Mouse a Cookie* by Laura Numeroff

- props listed below or LPs (pages 125–128)

  - an apron with four pockets

  - a real or plastic chocolate chip cookie

  - glass of fake milk

  - drinking straw

- cloth napkin

- small handheld mirror

- small scissors

- small handheld broom

- sponge

- dusting powder box that is empty

- small book (if possible use *If You Give a Mouse a Cookie)*

- crayons

- pen

- tape

- chart tablet or chalkboard and marker

- Mouse Minder Note (page 129)

Before Class

1. Put the items listed above into the four pockets of the apron in the order in which they appear in *If You Give a Mouse a Cookie*. If you are not using the items, follow the instructions from page 10 to create the LP visual for *If You Give a Mouse a Cookie*.

2. Practice telling the story using the items or LP pieces.

3. Copy a Mouse Minder Note for each child.

Lesson Plan

1. Tell *If You Give a Mouse a Cookie* by asking, "You know what?" and having the audience respond, "No, what?" with each action of the story. Draw the appropriate object out of your apron pocket as the story progresses. When the story is finished, put the objects out of sight before moving on to the next activity.

2. Urge the students to help you make a list of all the items the mouse asks for in the story. List these on a chart or chalkboard. If time permits, students can draw one of the objects for each item on the list. When the list is complete, highlight the following words: milk, cookie, scissors, crayons, tape, pen and sponge.

3. Use illustrations from the book to highlight reminders about caring for books: (a) show the picture of the mouse and the empty glass of milk to explain that the mouse needs food and drink but books do not; (b) show the picture of the mouse after he has cleaned the house to explain that both mice and books need to be clean, but books don't use water and soap; (c) share the illustrations that show the mouse using the scissors, crayons, pen and tape. Explain that the mouse needed them but books do not.

4. Ask if anyone remembers where the little boy put the mouse's picture in the story. Why did they pick the refrigerator as a good place to put the picture? Give each child a Mouse Minder Note to take home and put on his or her refrigerator. The note tells what day they are expected to return their library books.

Literature Pictures (LPs) for If You Give a Mouse a Cookie

Photocopy to desired size.

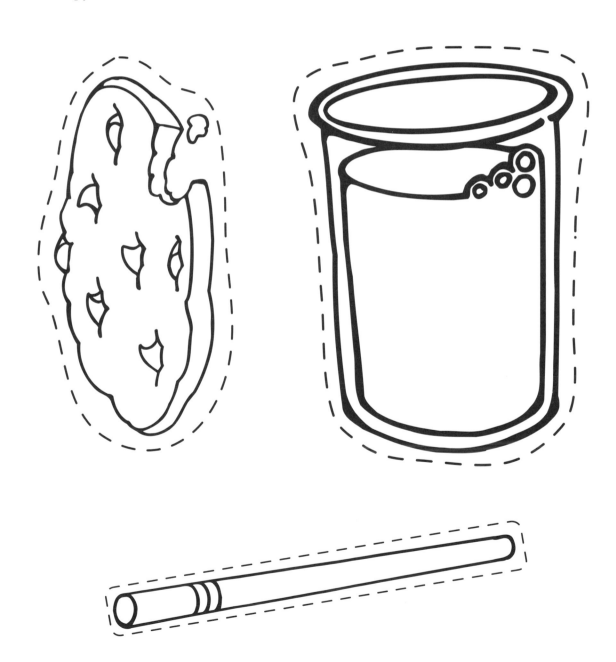

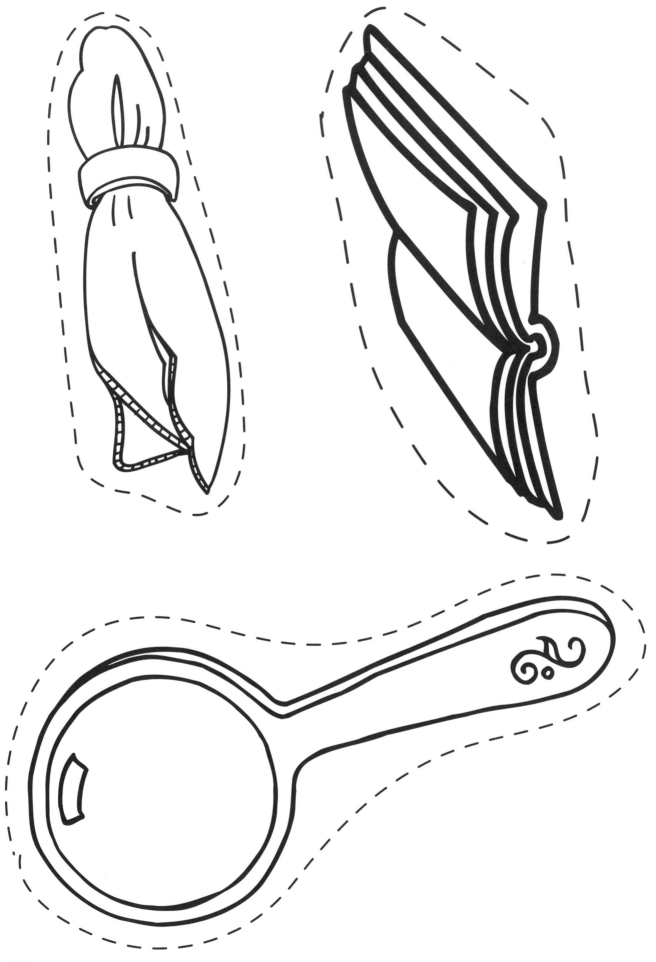

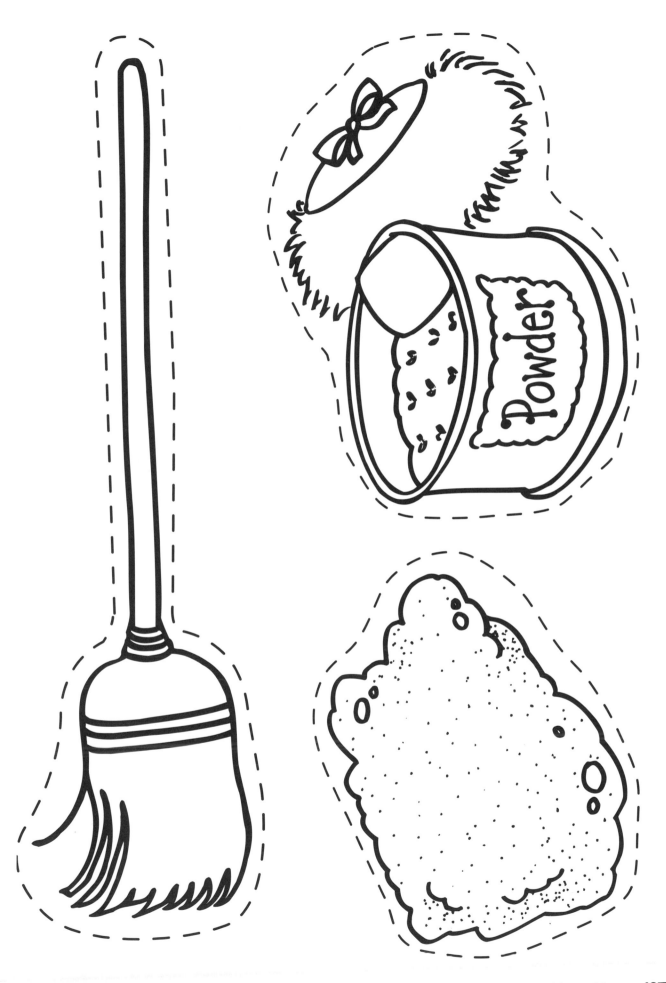

On the label: Powder

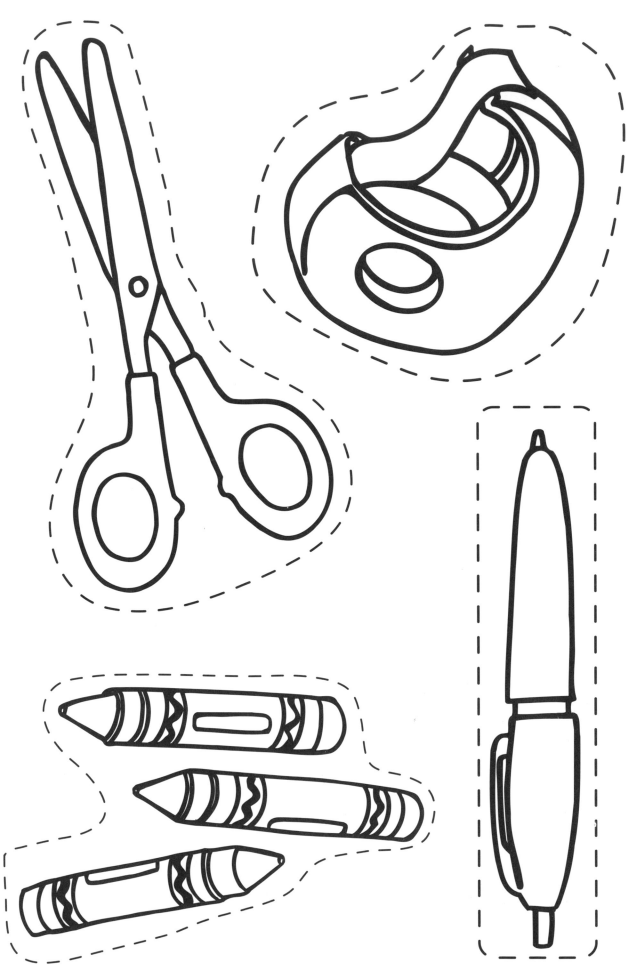

Mouse Minder says...

Remember

_____

is the day to return your book!

Mouse House • Lesson 4

Featured Book

Aesop's Fables by Jerry Pinkney. Chronicle Books, 2000.

A collection of nearly 60 fables from Aesop, including such familiar ones as "The Grasshopper and the Ants," "Androcles and the Lion," "The Lion and the Mouse" and "The North Wind and the Sun." ISBN 1587170000

Lesson Learning Ideas

Literature Appreciation

- Has had experience with various literary genres—fable

Techniques of Learning

- Is able to integrate cues from written and visual text

- Understands and participates in brainstorming activities

- Has established visual literacy skills

Comprehension

- Utilizes the comprehension strategy of prediction

Writing Experiences

- Is able to transfer ideas into sentences with appropriate support

- Responds to literature in a variety of written formats

- Can create labels, notes and/or captions

- Participates in descriptive writing experiences

- Has experience with examples of descriptive writing and its uses

Materials

- *Aesop's Fables* by Jerry Pinkney

- numerous books with captioned pictures

- chart paper and markers

Before Class

Gather numerous books that have captions for the pictures.

Lesson Plan

1. Show the picture that goes with "The Lion and the Mouse" story. Ask students to predict what this picture and the corresponding story might be about. Record the ideas students suggest.

2. Explain that today's story is a different kind of story called a fable. Share that fables are the oldest kind of known fiction. These stories are very short (in this case only one page long) and usually are about no more than three animals. In fables the animals talk and act like people but do not have personal names.

3. Read "The Lion and the Mouse."

4. Return to the picture. Ask the students if they want to add anything to their ideas about the picture.

5. Direct the students' attention to the pictures that have captions. Read several examples. Define captions for the students as phrases or sentences that tell about the picture and help with understanding the text. Have students locate captions in other books. Let them guess what the caption might say and then read aloud several of the captions.

6. Ask the students to help create a caption for the picture with today's fable. Use the list of ideas from earlier in the lesson.

7. Encourage students to think of captions (what pictures are about) whenever they read. This will help them be good readers.

Featured Book

Andy and the Lion by James Henry Daugherty. Puffin, 1989.

In this retelling of Androcles and the Lion, Andy meets a lion on the way to school and wins his friendship for life by removing a thorn from his paw. ISBN 0140502777

Lesson Learning Ideas

Library Skills

- Applies library manners

- Comprehends library management skills

- Can follow circulation procedures

- Can take proper care of books

Literature Appreciation

- Knows the meaning of award-winning literature

Techniques of Learning

- Can transfer learning experiences across multiple situations

Oral Language

- Is able to listen to and comprehend a variety of multimedia presentation formats

Materials

- *Andy and the Lion* by James Daugherty, book and video versions (see Ordering Information, page 188)

- copies of Great Rip Roar Read Report (page 134)

- several books—some damaged and some not damaged

- crayons

Before Class

1. Make multiple copies of the Great Rip Roar Read Report for students to see and color during class.

2. Gather examples of damaged and undamaged books.

3. Set up a location for the reports and damaged book return.

Lesson Plan

1. Inform the students that there is not a mouse in today's story but they may recognize a character who acts very much like the mouse in the fable from the last lesson.

   Note: This book is based on "Androcles and the Lion" but "The Lion and the Mouse" was substituted because it is more age appropriate.

2. Show the 11-minute *Andy and the Lion* video.

3. Introduce the Great Rip Roar Read Report to the students. Ask what sound a lion makes. Show the repair report form and share that the letters stand for the Great Rip Roar Read Report. Explain how they should look for books that need to be repaired before they check them out. Show examples of books that need to be repaired and explain how they will be fixed. Share books that do not need repair. Make sure the students understand the need to let the library staff repair books.

4. Explain how the library handles books that need repair. Set in place a procedure for students to check books for damage before checking them out. Let the children know that they should report damaged books by marking the form and placing it in the damaged book.

5. Let the students color one or more of the report forms. Then have them return the forms to their permanent location next to the place for damaged books.

Great Rip Roar Read Report

Pages torn

Pages missing

Written or colored in

Other

Name: _____

Featured Book

I. Q. Goes to the Library by Mary Ann Fraser. Walker & Co., 2003.

After going to the library with Mrs. Furber's class every day of Library Week, I. Q., the class pet, hopes to take out a funny book with his own library card. ISBN 0802788777

Lesson Learning Ideas

Library Skills

- Applies library manners

- Can select books based on personal interest

- Comprehends library management skills

- Can follow circulation procedures

- Can take proper care of books

Techniques of Learning

- Can transfer learning experiences across multiple situations

- Attends to personal and/or team tasks outside of the whole group setting

Comprehension

- Utilizes the comprehension strategy of prediction

Writing Experiences

- Has experience with examples of narrative writing and its uses

Materials

- *I. Q. Goes to the Library* by Mary Ann Fraser

- book bags for each student (see Ordering Information, page 188)

- parent letter (page 137)

- Bookmarks (page 138–139)

- crayons

Before Class

1. Make copies of the parent letter for each child. Give the principal a copy of the parent letter.

2. Make copies of the bookmarks on card stock for students to color.

3. Purchase or make book bags for student use.

Lesson Plan:

1. Start reading *I. Q. Goes to the Library.* Stop at the bottom of the second page of text and ask the children, "Who do you think I. Q. is? How is he a part of a class of school children?" Finish reading the book to the students.

2. Hand out the bookmarks while the children are still seated. Page through the book again and share the reminders on the bookmarks. One of the bookmark reminders is only on the endpapers. It says, "Let the librarian repair damaged library materials."

3. When students finish checking out their books (they will take them home today) let them color their bookmarks and the picture on their parent letter. Remind the children that library books are not coloring books.

4. Read the parent letter aloud so the students understand the content. As the children line up, place their book, bookmark and letter in a book bag. Lead the children in the following chant: "Remember to bring your book and your book bag back!"

Dear Parents,

Today is a big day!

Your child has practiced how to care for and check out books and is bringing home his or her first library book today. We hope this is the beginning of something very special in your child's life.

We can't do it all—we need your help! You can help ensure that checking out library books is an enjoyable experience if you help your child with the following:

1. Read the book with your child and talk about the story.

2. Encourage your child to have a special "home" for his or her book so that it will not get lost or damaged.

3. Remind your child of the proper way to handle books.

4. Support your child's efforts to return library books on time.

If your child loses or damages a book beyond repair, library policy states that the book will need to be paid for so other children will have the same chance to enjoy library books.

Most important of all—please **READ, READ, READ!**

Sincerely,

A book bag is a must to protect books from rain, dirt, and dust.

To keep books neat, don't eat or drink when you read.

Save your place without a trace— use a bookmark.

To keep books looking new, never mark, cut, draw, or glue.

Return or renew when your book is due.

A whispering voice is the best choice.

shhhhhh

Farmyard Friends

Farmyard Friends · Lesson 1

Featured Book

Petunia by Roger Duvoisin. Knopf, 2000.

A silly goose carries around a book she thinks will make her wise.
ISBN 0394808657

Lesson Learning Ideas

Techniques of Learning

- Understands and participates in brainstorming activities

- Attends to personal and/or team tasks outside of the whole group setting

- Is able to integrate cues from written and visual text

- Has established visual literacy skills

Comprehension

- Has extended personal vocabulary

Writing Experiences

- Has participated in a variety of age-appropriate writing experiences

- Responds to literature in a variety of written formats

- Uses prewriting strategies such as drawing, brainstorming and/or graphic organizers

- Participates in descriptive writing experiences

- Has experience with examples of descriptive writing and its uses

Materials

- *Petunia* by Roger Duvoisin

- crayons

- handmade story pieces of Petunia (see Ordering Information, page 188) or video (see Ordering Information, page 188)

- 26 blank pages with one letter of the alphabet on each

- alphabet books from the library collection

- other Petunia books

Before Class

1. If you are using the story pieces, make them into metal board or Velcro apron pieces. Do this by backing the pieces with magnets or Velcro.

2. Copy the alphabet pages so there will be enough for each child to have one.

3. Locate all of the Petunia books from the library collection.

Lesson Plan

1. Read *Petunia*. (This is a very old book but it is back in print.) Enhance the telling by using the handmade story pieces or the video.

2. At the end of the story, Petunia tries to learn to read by reading an alphabet book. Introduce some of the alphabet books in your collection and allow students time to read several alphabet books.

3. Have the children create their own class alphabet book from *Petunia*. The children should search by letter to find words in the story that begin with each letter of the alphabet. Start the search using the characters in the story. Then move to objects and actions. Once words are found, the children can draw pictures based on the story for each word. Some examples from *Petunia* are:

A: advice	N: nine
B: book	O: opinion
C: Clover the cow	P: Petunia
D: dog named Noisy	Q:
E: exploded	R: red comb or read
F: fire or firecrackers	S: six or sad
G: goose	T: toothache
H: horse named Straw	U: understand
I: Ida, the hen	V:
J: jerked his head out of the hole	W: wise or wisdom
K: King, the rooster	X:
L: lays eggs or lost chicks	Y:
M: Mr. Pumpkin	Z:

Notice that not all of the letters can be found. Either let the children come up with words that might fit the story for those letters or leave them blank. Bind the pictures together in book form. Have the students create a title and author entry for the cover.

4. Introduce the other Petunia books.

Farmyard Friends · Lesson 2

Featured Book

Book! Book! Book! by Deborah Bruss. Scholastic, 2001.

When the children go back to school, the animals on the farm are bored so they go into the library in town trying to find something to do.
ISBN 0439135257

Lesson Learning Ideas

Techniques of Learning

- Has experience in critical thinking questioning

- Has the opportunity to work in cooperative groups

- Understands and participates in brainstorming activities

- Is able to integrate cues from written and visual text

- Uses organizational formats for learning

- Can transfer learning experiences across multiple situations

- Attends to personal and/or team tasks outside of the whole group setting

Comprehension

- Has experience in the comprehension strategy of retelling

- Can recall, summarize and paraphrase what is listened to and viewed

Materials

- *Book! Book! Book!* by Deborah Bruss

- Farm Animal Pictures (page 147)

- Finger Puppet Patterns (page 148, or Ordering Information, page 189)

- Table of Animal Information (pages 149–150)

Before Class

1. Copy a set of farm animal pictures to use for charades.

2. Make a set of finger puppets to use in reading *Book! Book! Book!*

2. Copy the Table of Animal Information

Lesson Plan

1. Play a game of Farmyard Charades. Take turns showing one student a picture of a farm animal and having him or her make the sound that animal makes. The person who guesses correctly takes the next turn.

2. Explain to the students that today's book is about the sounds farm animals make. Read aloud *Book! Book! Book!* and/or use the finger puppets to tell the story.

3. Tell the children that they are going to help create a puzzle about the animals in the story. Show the table and read the headings. Tell the students that this "puzzle picture" is called a table. Explain that a table is a way to organize or group information.

4. Ask the children to list all of the animals in the story. As each animal is mentioned, place its name and picture on the table. Use the first animal in the table and share the information that fits in each column. Model where you found the information for each category. Then read one story segment at a time and have the children decide what should be placed in each column. **Note:** The frog is pictured on every page but does not appear in the text until the last two pages. The duck appears at the beginning of the story but does not enter the library. The mouse is pictured on most, but not all, of the pages and is never mentioned in the text.

5. If the duck, frog or mouse are listed, have the children discuss why they think they were treated as they were in the story. Duck, Frog and Mouse do not have all of the needed information in the text of the story (see page 150 for suggestions). Fill in all that is known and then let the children create the rest.

6. When the table is complete, review the information. If time permits, allow the students to play another version of Farmyard Charades. Divide the students into pairs and model how to play. Have one partner say one of the items from the table. For example, one person might say "clip-clopped." His or her partner then tries to guess the animal the item goes with. Both students get a point when the question is answered correctly. Play moves back and forth between partners.

Farm Animal Pictures

Photocopy to desired size.

Table of Animal Information

Name and picture of animal	Beginning sound description (adverb alliteration)	How the animal walked into the library	The sound the animal made

Table of Animal Information

Name and picture of animal	Beginning sound description (adverb alliteration)	How the animal walked into the library	The sound the animal made
horse	hung his head	clip-clopped	neigh
cow	complained	plodded in	moo
goat	grumbled	trotted in	baaah
pig	pouted	ambled in	oink
hen	heaved a sigh	flapped	book book
duck	dozed off	waddled along	quack
frog	frowned fiercely	hopped	read-it
mouse	muttered to himself	tiptoed	squeak

Farmyard Friends · Lesson 3

Featured Book

Wolf! by Becky Bloom. Scholastic, 1999.

A wolf learns to read in order to impress a group of farmyard animals he has met. ISBN 0531301559

Lesson Learning Ideas

Techniques of Learning

- Has established visual literacy skills

- Has experience in critical thinking questioning

- Uses organizational formats for learning

- Can transfer learning experiences across multiple situations

- Attends to personal and/or team tasks outside of the whole group setting

Comprehension

- Has extended personal vocabulary

- Utilizes the comprehension strategy of prediction

- Is able to make connections with prior knowledge and experience

Materials

- *Wolf!* by Becky Bloom

- video of *Wolf!* (see Ordering Information, page 189)

- Vocabulary Worksheet (page 153)

Before Class

Make a copy of the vocabulary page for each student.

Lesson Plan

1. Show the seven-minute *Wolf!* video.

2. After the video, read aloud the text from the third page of the book that begins "...and leaped at the animals with a _____." Ask the students to describe how the duck, cow

and pig felt or acted toward the wolf the first time they met him. If the children do not use the word "ignore" from the text, add it to their description. Explain that when you ignore something or someone you do not notice or pay attention.

3. Show the last page in the book. Ask the children how the duck, cow and pig felt or acted toward the wolf at the end of the story. If the children do not use the word "admire" from earlier in the story, introduce it as part of the description. Explain that when you admire someone, you really like that person or wish you were like him or her.

4. Display the two focus words for the students to see. Help the students think about the words by sharing things you wish others would ignore about you and things you wish others would admire about you. Allow students to share ideas of things they wish would be ignored or admired.

5. During free reading time give each child the vocabulary page. Instruct the children to draw things in two of the boxes that they wish would be ignored about them. In the other two boxes they should draw two things they wish people admired about them.

Ignore and Admire
Vocabulary Sheet

I wish _____
would ignore _____
_____.

I wish _____
would admire _____
_____.

I wish _____
would ignore _____
_____.

I wish _____
would admire _____
_____.

Featured Books

Brown Bear, Brown Bear, What Do You See? by Eric Carle. Henry Holt & Company, 1983.

Children see a variety of animals, each one a different color, and a teacher looking at them. ISBN 0805017445

I Went Walking by Sue Williams. Harcourt, 1990.

During the course of a walk, a young boy identifies animals of different colors. ISBN 0152004718

Let's Go Visiting by Sue Williams. Harcourt, 1998.

A counting story in which a boy visits his farmyard friends, from one brown foal to six yellow puppies. ISBN 0152018239

Lesson Learning Ideas

Techniques of Learning

- Has established visual literacy skills

- Has experience with compare and contrast questioning

- Is able to integrate cues from written and visual text

- Understands and participates in brainstorming activities

- Uses organizational formats for learning

- Can transfer learning experiences across multiple situations

Comprehension

- Has the opportunity to participate in experiences that support the acquisition of fluency

Writing Experiences

- Has participated in a variety of age-appropriate writing experiences

- Is able to generate brief descriptions that use sensory details

- Responds to literature in a variety of written formats

- Imitates models of good writing

- Participates in descriptive writing experiences
- Has experience with examples of descriptive writing and its uses

Materials

- *Brown Bear, Brown Bear, What Do You See?* by Eric Carle
- *I Went Walking* big book, by Sue Williams (see Ordering Information, page 189)
- *Let's Go Visiting* by Sue Williams
- LPs for both featured books (pages 156–160)
- writing frames (pages 161–163)
- metal board

Before Class

1. Make the *Let's Go Visiting* LPs into a metal board presentation. Follow the instructions from page 10 to create the LPs.

2. Make multiple copies of the writing frames.

3. Make multiple sets of the LPs for *I Went Walking* and *Let's Go Visiting* for students to use to retell the stories. These sets can be used for free reading materials.

Lesson Plan

1. Advise the students that today's first book has clues to the story hidden in the pictures. Read aloud the big book version of *I Went Walking*. Divide the class into two groups, then read the book again. Have group one read, "I went walking," and group two read, "What did you see?" Then the whole class should read the response.

2. Discuss the clues in the pictures. Ask the students if the story makes them think of other stories they have read. When students have had an opportunity to share their ideas and reasons, introduce *Brown Bear, Brown Bear*. If students don't know this story share it with them. Then discuss how the books are alike and different.

3. Tell *Let's Go Visiting* using a metal board presentation. (Both stories provide an excellent way to practice color recognition and color words. This story can also be used to practice numbers and number words to six.) Ask the children how the stories are alike.

4. Have the children use the writing frames on pages 161–162. (A blank writing frame is included on page 163 if you would like to make your own writing frame.) Have the children illustrate their work. Put all of the pages together to make a class book for the free reading collection.

Literature Pictures (LPs) for I Went Walking

Photocopy to desired size.

Photocopy to desired size.

I went walking.

What did you

see? I saw a

looking at me.

Let's go visiting.

What did you

say?

(is) (are) ready

to play.

Farmyard Friends • Lesson 5

Featured Book

Click, Clack, Moo: Cows That Type by Doreen Cronin. Simon & Schuster, 2000.

When Farmer Brown's cows find a typewriter in the barn they start making demands and go on strike when the farmer refuses to give them what they want. ISBN 0689832133

Lesson Learning Ideas

Literature Appreciation

- Is familiar with the concept of a sequel

- Knows the meaning of award-winning literature

Comprehension

- Has extended personal vocabulary

Oral Language

- Has taken part in storytelling and read aloud experiences

Materials

- *Click, Clack, Moo: Cows That Type* big book or video, by Doreen Cronin (see Ordering Information, page 189)

- *Giggle, Giggle, Quack* by Doreen Cronin (Simon & Schuster, 2002)

- *Duck for President* by Doreen Cronin (Simon & Schuster, 2004)

Before Class

Nothing needed.

Lesson Plan

1. Ask if anyone knows what a typewriter is. Show the picture of one from the title page of the big book. Explain that it was like an early computer before there were computers. Share *Click, Clack, Moo: Cows That Type* by showing the 10-minute video.

2. Tell the students that they are going to have a chance to help read the story. Use the big book for this part of the lesson. Divide the class into three sections. One section will say "click" or "clickety." The second section will say "clack." And the last group

will say "moo." As you read, point to the groups to cue their help. For an added component, have the students stand and raise their hands over their heads as they repeat their word (like the wave at a football game). Remind students that the words vary from time to time in the story so they should watch and listen carefully.

3. Introduce the following words based on the story: strike, compromise and ultimatum. Before going into the meaning of the words ask the students: "What was the problem in the story?" Once the children understand the problem or disagreement in the story tell them that the words all have to do with ways to try to solve a disagreement.

4. Reread the part of the story that includes the word "strike." Explain to the children that to strike means to refuse to work. Ask: Who refused to work in the story? What happened because of the strike? Did going on strike solve the problem?

5. Move to the word "ultimatum." Reread the part of the story that includes this word. Explain that an ultimatum is a final word or demand. Ask: What was the ultimatum? Who set the ultimatum? Did the ultimatum solve the problem?

6. Introduce the word "compromise." This word does not appear in the text of the story but the concept does. Read the last note in the book. Share with the students that this is a compromise. A compromise is usually an action in which the two groups disagreeing both get something in order to solve the problem. Ask: Did the compromise solve the problem?

7. Be sure to show the picture at the end of the story. What new problem did Farmer Brown have at the end of the story? Ask the children how they think the ducks got a diving board. Did they use a strike, an ultimatum and/or a compromise?

8. Then share *Giggle, Giggle, Quack*. Explain to the children the concept of a sequel. *Duck for President* is another book in the series.

Farmyard Friends · Lesson 6

Featured Books

Ah-Choo! **by Margery Cuyler. Scholastic, 2002.**

A sneeze spreads from a farmer to his wife to various animals on the farm until they are all in bed with the flu. ISBN 0439266181

Barnyard Song **by Rhonda Greene. Simon & Schuster, 1997.**

When the barnyard animals catch the flu, the farmer takes care of them until their usual voices return. ISBN 0689807589

Farm Flu **by Teresa Bateman. Albert Whitman, 2001.**

When the farm animals seem to catch the flu one after another, a young boy does his best to take care of them. ISBN 0807522740

Where the Sidewalk Ends **by Shel Silverstein. HarperCollins, 1973.**

A boy who turns into a TV set and a girl who eats a whale are only two of the characters in a collection of humorous poetry illustrated with the author's own drawings. ISBN 0060256672

Note: These are excellent books to send home to a child who has an extended illness.

Lesson Learning Ideas

Literature Appreciation

- Has had experience with various literary genres—poetry

Techniques of Learning

- Has the opportunity to work in cooperative groups

- Attends to personal and/or team tasks outside of the whole group setting

- Understands and participates in brainstorming activities

Comprehension

- Has experience in the comprehension strategy of retelling

- Has an opportunity to participate in experiences that support the acquisition of fluency

- Is able to set a purpose for reading

- Can recall, summarize and paraphrase what is listened to and viewed

Oral Language

- Has taken part in storytelling and read aloud experiences

- Is able to listen to and comprehend a variety of multimedia presentation formats

- Is developing the ability to respond to what is seen and heard

Materials

- *Ah-Choo!* by Margery Cuyler (several copies)

- *Barnyard Song* by Rhonda Greene (several copies)

- *Farm Flu* by Teresa Bateman (several copies)

- *Where the Sidewalk Ends* by Shel Silverstein

- chalkboard or chart tablet

- Listening Centers, read along tapes and multiple copies of featured books

- get well cards *(optional)*

Before Class

1. Create a read-along tape to go with each of the featured books.

2. If possible, gather three listening centers to use for the lesson.

3. Create a farm animal concentration game. See step 5 of the Lesson Plan. *(optional)*

4. Gather get well cards. *(optional)*

Lesson Plan

1. Read aloud the poem "Sick" from *Where the Sidewalk Ends*. Ask the children how the girl in the poem got over being sick.

2. Suggest that the children think about a time when they were sick in bed. Make a class list of things someone did for the students to try to make them feel better.

3. Divide the students into three groups for listening. Share with them that each group will listen to a different story about farm animals and being sick.

4. After listening to the story, ask the children to form new groups. In the new groups there should be one child who listened to each of the books. In the groups announce one book at a time and have the student who listened to that story tell the others about it. Continue until all three stories have been shared.

5. If time permits, bring in numerous get well cards for students to use as examples and have them create their own get well card for one of the animals in the story. Or, create a farm animal concentration game using the pictures from lesson 2 and the instructions from Stories in Threes, lesson 6.

Farmyard Friends · Lesson 7

Lesson Learning Ideas

Literature Appreciation

• Has used fiction and nonfiction materials

Techniques of Learning

• Has established visual literacy skills

• Has experience in critical thinking questioning

• Has the opportunity to work in cooperative groups

• Understands and participates in brainstorming activities

• Is able to integrate cues from written and visual text

• Uses organizational formats for learning

• Attends to personal and/or team tasks outside the whole group setting

• Takes an active role in recomposing visual and written information

Comprehension

• Can recall, summarize and paraphrase what is listened to and viewed

Materials

• all of the featured books from the unit

• Farm Animal Table (pages 170–171)

• Farm Animal Graph (page 172)

• Farm Animal Pictures (page 173)

Before Class

1. Make a transparency or poster size copy of the Farm Animal Table so it can be used by the entire class.

2. Make copies of the Farm Animal Table for each group.

3. Create a class size copy of the Farm Animal Graph and nine copies of each animal picture to use on the graph.

Lesson Plan

1. Display all of the books and ask the class to help remember the names of the books read. Go over the animals listed to make sure the students can see the pictures. Select one book from the unit and as a class identify the farm animals that appear in the book. Show the students how to mark the table to indicate the animals from the selected book.

2. Divide the students into groups (four groups with two books each or eight groups with one book each). Instruct the groups to "read" the pictures in their book(s) and mark on the group table for each farm animal that is part of their book.

3. Gather the children back into a whole class setting. Call out the name of each animal on the table. As each animal is called have the groups indicate if that animal appeared in their book. Continue to gather the group information until all of the animals have been accounted for.

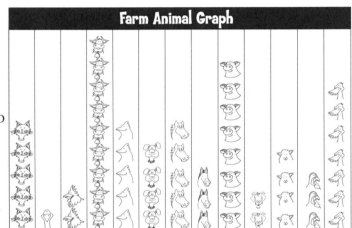

4. Have the students count to see how many times each animal appears in the books. Demonstrate how to transfer the information to a graph. Use pictures of the animals to create a picture graph in bar graph form.

5. Ask the students questions that they need to use information from the graph in order to answer.

Sample questions:

- Which animal(s) appeared in the most stories? (cow)

- Which animal(s) appeared in the least stories? (goose)

- Which appeared in more stories—the goose or the dog? (dog)

- Which appeared in fewer stories—the horse or the turkey? (turkey)

- Which book had the most animals? (*Petunia*)

- Which book had the least animals? (*Wolf!* and *Click, Clack, Moo*)

- What book(s) did not have a pig? (*Click, Clack, Moo*)

- Next to the cow, which animal appeared in the most stories? (pig)

Farm Animal Table

	Petunia	Wolf	I Went Walking	Let's Go Visiting	Click, Clack, Moo	Farm Flu	Book! Book! Book!	Ah-Choo	Barnyard Song
cat									
goose									
rooster									
cow									
hen/chicken									
dog									
horse									
donkey									
pig									
goat									
sheep									
turkey									
duck									

Farm Animal Table

	Petunia	Wolf	I Went Walking	Let's Go Visiting	Click, Clack, Moo	Farm Flu	Book! Book! Book!	Ah-Choo	Barnyard Song
cat	X		X	X				X	X
goose	X								
rooster	X								X
cow	X	X	X	X	X	X	X	X	X
hen/chicken	X				X	X	X	X	
dog	X		X	X				X	
horse	X		X	X			X		X
donkey	X					X			X
pig	X	X	X	X		X	X	X	X
goat	X					X			
sheep	X					X		X	X
turkey	X					X			X
duck	X	X	X	X	X		X		X

Farm Animal Graph

Farm Animal Pictures

cat

chicken/hen

cow

dog

donkey

duck

goat

goose

horse

pig

rooster

sheep

turkey

Farmyard Friends • Lesson 8

Featured Books

Chickens by Rachael Bell. Heinemann Library, 2000.

Introduces this farm animal, exploring birth, growth, living conditions and uses of the chicken. ISBN 1575725304

Cows by Rachael Bell. Heinemann Library, 2000.

Describes the habits and behavior of cows and how they are kept and cared for on a dairy farm. ISBN 1575725290

Horses by Rachael Bell. Heinemann Library, 2000.

Introduces this farm animal, exploring birth, growth, living conditions and uses of the horse. ISBN 1575725312

Pigs by Rachael Bell. Heinemann Library, 2000.

Introduces this farm animal by describing its physical appearance, manner of reproduction, eating and sleeping habits, ways of staying healthy, required care and uses. ISBN 1575725320

Sheep by Rachael Bell. Heinemann Library, 2000.

Introduces this farm animal by describing its physical appearance, manner of reproduction, eating and sleeping habits, ways of staying healthy, required care and uses. ISBN 1575725339

Turkeys by Rachael Bell. Heinemann Library, 2000.

Introduces this farm animal by describing its physical appearance, manner of reproduction, eating and roosting habits, ways of staying healthy, required care and uses. ISBN 1575725347

Lesson Learning Ideas

Literature Appreciation

- Has used fiction and nonfiction materials
- Has an initial understanding of the difference between fiction and nonfiction

Techniques of Learning

- Has experience with compare and contrast questioning
- Uses organizational formats for learning

Comprehension

- Is beginning to comprehend basic text structures
- Has extended personal vocabulary

Writing Experiences

- Uses prewriting strategies such as drawings, brainstorming and/or graphic organizers

Materials

- nonfiction books on farm animals (see featured books, Ordering Information, page 189)
- Venn Diagram (page 176)

Before Class

Photocopy a class size Venn diagram to use with this lesson.

Lesson Plan

1. Hand out books from the Farm Animals series by Heinemann. The books in this series include: *Pigs, Chickens, Sheep, Cows, Turkeys* and *Horses.* Encourage the children to look at these books to decide how they compare to the other books from this unit.

2. Create a Venn diagram to compare the Farm Animal books with the other books from the unit.

3. Re-introduce the concept of nonfiction that was talked about in Teddy Bear Time. Remind students that we read nonfiction in a different way than we read fiction. Fiction is read from beginning to end and nonfiction is usually read in segments based on desire for information.

4. Read aloud the chapter called "Raising Horses," pages 20–21 from *Horses,* and the chapter "Other Sheep Farms," pages 24–25 in *Sheep.*

5. Direct the students' attention to the bold-faced words within the text. Explain that these are important words that the author thought a reader might not understand. These highlighted words appear in the glossary at the back of the book. Ask students what they think each word means. Check their understanding against the information contained in the glossary.

6. If time permits, take student requests for chapters to read aloud. Explain that this is an example of how you read nonfiction—based on interest and need to know.

Venn Diagram

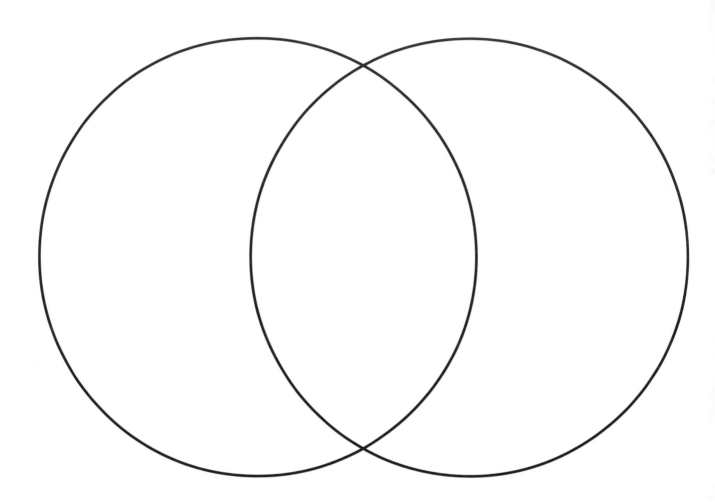

Featured Book

Cows by Rachael Bell. Heinemann Library, 2000.

Describes the habits and behavior of cows and how they are kept and cared for on a dairy farm. ISBN 1575725290

Taking Care of Farm Animals by Dimi Stanos. National Geographic Society, 2002.

A wordless book that shows the types of care needed for different animals. ISBN 0792284828

Lesson Learning Ideas

Literature Appreciation

- Has used fiction and nonfiction materials

- Has an initial understanding of the difference between fiction and nonfiction

Techniques of Learning

- Is able to integrate cues from written and visual text

- Takes an active role in recomposing visual and written information

Comprehension

- Is able to make connections with prior knowledge and experience

- Can recall, summarize and paraphrase what is listened to and viewed

- Is beginning to comprehend basic text structures

Writing Experiences

- Has participated in a variety of age-appropriate writing experiences

- Can create labels, notes and/or captions

- Uses prewriting strategies such as drawings, brainstorming and/or graphic organizers

- Is able to transfer ideas into sentences with appropriate support

- Participates in descriptive writing experiences

Materials

- *Taking Care of Farm Animals* by Dimi Stanos
- *Cows* by Rachael Bell
- graph from lesson 7 (page 172)
- chart
- markers
- caption pages (pages 179–183)

Before Class

1. Post the graph created in lesson 7.
2. Copy enough caption pages so each child will have one.

Lesson Plan

1. Direct the students' attention to the graph. Ask the children if they remember the animal that has appeared in the most fiction books in this unit (cow). Explain that they will now investigate nonfiction books about cows. Ask the children to define nonfiction.

2. Read aloud the chapter "Raising Cows," pages 20–21 from *Cows*. Take a few student requests for other chapters to read aloud.

3. Revisit the idea of bold-faced words and glossary information using the text selection for this lesson.

4. Introduce *Taking Care of Farm Animals*. Turn the pages and ask the students what a book with only pictures is called (wordless). Focus attention on the page with the cow. Ask questions to get students talking about the veterinarian in the picture.

5. Have the students brainstorm about the content of the picture. Together, create a caption for the picture.

6. Reverse the previous activity by giving students one of the caption pages. Read each caption aloud and discuss them with the class. Allow time for each student to create a picture to go with their caption.

Doctors who take care of animals are called veterinarians or vets.

Veterinarians who care for farm animals are called large animal vets.

Farm animals can get sick just like people.

Vets give cows shots (vaccinations) to keep them healthy.

Sometimes veterinarians go to farms to take care of their animal patients.

Lesson Learning Ideas

Literature Appreciation

- Has used fiction and nonfiction materials

- Has an initial understanding of the difference between fiction and nonfiction

Techniques of Learning

- Is able to integrate cues from written and visual text

- Takes an active role in recomposing visual and written information

- Has established visual literacy skills

- Attends to personal and/or team tasks outside of the whole group setting

Comprehension

- Is able to make connections with prior knowledge and experience

- Can recall, summarize and paraphrase what is listened to and viewed

- Is beginning to comprehend basic text structures

Writing Experiences

- Has participated in a variety of age-appropriate writing experiences

- Can create labels, notes and/or captions

- Uses prewriting strategies such as drawings, brainstorming and/or graphic organizers

- Is able to transfer ideas into sentences with appropriate support

- Participates in descriptive writing experiences

Materials

- *Pigs* by Rachael Bell
- *Taking Care of Farm Animals* by Dimi Stanos
- other books from your collection on pigs (see suggestions below)
- graph from lesson 7 (page 172)
- writing and drawing materials
- chart and markers

Before Class

Post the graph created in lesson 7.

Lesson Plan

1. Ask the students to return to the graph from lesson 7. The cow was in the most books from the unit. What animal was in second place? (Pig.) Share that today's lesson will focus on nonfiction information about pigs.

2. Read aloud the chapter "Where Do Pigs Live?" pages 12–13 of *Pigs*. Revisit the idea of bold-faced words and glossary information using the text selection for this lesson.

3. Divide the children into groups to look in books for pictures about where pigs live. Give the student groups time to look for pictures in the books from the library collection.

4. Bring the class back together and have the students share the pictures they found. Create a brainstorm list of words and phrases to describe where pigs live. Ask the children to pick words that they think should be bold-faced words and create definitions for each word.

5. Allow the students to work in pairs or alone to create a picture about pigs. They can draw a picture with a caption of where pigs live that might fit into *Taking Care of Farm Animals*, or they can use a bold-faced word with a definition and create a drawing to illustrate the concept.

Booklist of Pig Books

- *All Pigs are Beautiful* by Dick King-Smith. Candlewick Press, 2001.
- *A Day at Greenhill Farm* by Sue Nicholson. DK Publishing, 1998.
- *From Piglet to Pig* by Jillian Powell. Raintree Publishers, 2002.
- *Life on a Pig Farm* by Judy Wolfman. Lerner Publishing Group, 2001.
- *Pig* by Jules Older. Charlesbridge Publishing, 2004.
- *Pigs* by Peter Brady. Capstone Press, 1996.
- *Pigs* by Gail Gibbons. Holiday House, 1999.

- *Pigs* by Ann Larkin Hansen. Checkerboard Books, 1998.
- *Pigs* by Cynthia F. Klingel. Child's World Inc., 2000.
- *Pigs* by Julie Murray. ABDO Publishing Co., 2002.

Web sites to Use

- Kids Farm *www.kidsfarm.com/wheredo.htm*
- Farm Animal Resources *www.kiddyhouse.com/Farm/*

❀ Ordering Information ❀

Teddy Bear Time

Lesson 2

Corduroy Video: Available from Weston Woods. Item number WMPV436VCC for $49.95.

> Weston Woods
> 143 Main Street
> Norwalk, CT 06851
> 800-243-5020
> Fax 203-845-0498
> _www.scholastic.com/westonwoods_

Lesson 3

A Pocket for Corduroy Read-Along Cassette: ISBN 0140951245 available from Barnes and Noble (_www.bn.com_) and Amazon.com for under $10.00. Individual paperback copies of the book are available from Scholastic. Item number LBD31970 at $3.95 each.

Corduroy Stamps: Available from Kidstamps. Corduroy stamps come in two different sizes— item 1753 is a ½″ x 1″ stamp for $5.00 and item 593 is a 1″ x 2″ stamp for $6.50.

> Kidstamps
> P.O. Box 18699
> Cleveland Hts, OH 44118
> 800-727-5437
> Fax 216-291-6887
> _www.kidstamps.com_

Lesson 4

Where's My Teddy Big Book: Available from Follett Library Resources or Barnes and Noble. ISBN 1564024687.

> Follett Library Resources
> 1340 Ridgeview Drive
> McHenry, IL 60050
> 888-511-5114
> Fax 800-852-5458
> www.flr.follett.com

Five-Section Sorting Boxes: Available from _www.highsmith.com_. Item number 68112.

Lesson 5

Metal Boards: 15″ x 20″ metal boards (code 38) are available from Keep the Story Going.

> Keep the Story Going
> 3641 Trousdale Lane
> Columbia, TN 38401
> 800-615-5860
> _www.keepthestorygoing.com_

Storytelling Aprons: Available from Lakeshore Learning Materials for $19.95 plus shipping and handling.

> Lakeshore Learning Materials
> 2695 E. Dominguez St.
> P.O. Box 6261
> Carson, CA 90895
> 800-421-5354
> _www.lakeshorelearning.com_

Lesson 7

The Teddy Bear Factory Video: Available from Library Video Company (public performance rights included). The item number is K0571 and the price is $14.95.

> Library Video Company
> P.O. Box 580
> Wynnewood, PA 19096
> 800-843-3620
> Fax 610-645-4040
> _www.libraryvideo.com_

Stories in Threes

Lesson 2

Goldilocks Returns Video: Available from Spoken Arts for $49.95. Item number 9657.

> Spoken Arts
> 195 South White Rock Road
> Holmes, NY 12531
> 800-326-4090
> Fax 845-878-9009
> _www.spokenartsmedia.com_

Same-Different Fairy Tales: Available from Kagan Cooperative Learning. It can be purchased for $12 or in combination with _Same-Different Holidays_ for $20.

> Kagan Cooperative Learning
> P.O. Box 72008
> San Clemente, CA 92673
> 800-933-2667
> Fax 949-369-6311
> _www.kaganonline.com_

Lesson 5

Same-Different Fairy Tales: See above.

Out Foxed

Lesson 1

Wings: A Tale of Two Chickens Video: Available from Weston Woods for $49.95.

> Weston Woods
> 143 Main Street
> Norwalk, CT 06851
> 800-243-5020
> Fax 203-845-0498
> _www.scholastic.com/westonwoods_

Lesson 2

Rosie's Walk Big Book: Available from Scholastic Books, item number LDB64786 for $24.95.

> Scholastic Books
> 2931 E. McCarty Street
> Jefferson City, MO 65101
> 800-724-6527
> Fax 800-560-6815
> _www.scholastic.com_

Rosie and the Fox Stamps: Available from Kidstamps. Rosie is item number 369 for $6 and the fox is item number 370 for $6.50.

> Kidstamps
> P.O. Box 18699
> Cleveland Hts, OH 44118
> 800-727-5437
> Fax 216-291-6887
> _www.kidstamps.com_

Lesson 4

The Tale of Tricky Fox Video: Available from Spoken Arts for a cost of $49.95. The item number is SAV9668.

> Spoken Arts
> 195 South White Rock Road
> Holmes, NY 12531
> 800-326-4090
> Fax 845-878-9009
> _www.spokenartsmedia.com_

Mouse House

Lesson 5

Andy and the Lion Video: Available from Weston Woods/Scholastic for $49.95 under item number WMPV009V.

> Weston Woods
> 143 Main Street
> Norwalk, CT 06851
> 800-243-5020
> Fax 203-845-0498
> _www.scholastic.com/westonwoods_

Lesson 6

Plastic Book Bags: Available from Highsmith (_www.highsmith.com_).

Farmyard Friends

Lesson 1

Petunia Story Pieces: Available from Beulah's Creations for $30.

> Beulah Martinkus
> 1615 South 22nd, Apartment 14
> Fort Smith, AR 72901
> 501-783-5741

Petunia Video: Available from Weston Woods under item number WMPV045VCC for $49.95.

> Weston Woods
> 143 Main Street
> Norwalk, CT 06851
> 800-243-5020
> Fax 203-845-0498
> _www.scholastic.com/westonwoods_

Lesson 2

Book! Book! Book! Finger Puppets: Available from Merry Hearts. The 4″ finger puppets are item number FSS2 and sell for $28.99.

> Merry Hearts
> P.O. Box 158
> 735 E. Hampton Street
> Olanta, SC 29114
> 800-675-1766
> Fax 845-396-4527
> *www.merryhearts.com*

Lesson 3

Wolf! Video: Available from Spoken Arts. The item is number 9497 and it is $49.95.

> Spoken Arts
> 195 South White Rock Road
> Holmes, NY 12531
> 800-326-4090
> Fax 845-878-9009
> *www.spokenartsmedia.com*

Lesson 4

I Went Walking Big Book: Available from Follett Library Resources. The item is 10337D7 and it sells for $22.00.

> Follett Library Resources
> 1340 Ridgeview Drive
> McHenry, IL 60050
> 888-511-5114
> Fax 800-852-5458
> www.flr.follett.com

Metal Boards: 15″ x 20″ metal boards (code 38) are available from Keep the Story Going.

> Keep the Story Going
> 3641 Trousdale Lane
> Columbia, TN 38401
> 800-615-5860
> *www.keepthestorygoing.com*

Lesson 5

Click, Clack, Moo Big Book: Available from Scholastic Books. The item number is NTS944210 and it is $24.95.

> Scholastic Books
> 2931 E. McCarty Street
> Jefferson City, MO 65101
> 800-724-6527
> Fax 800-560-6815
> *www.scholastic.com*

Click, Clack, Moo Video: Available from Weston Woods for $60 for the English version and $29.95 for the Spanish version.

> Weston Woods
> 143 Main Street
> Norwalk, CT 06851
> 800-243-5020
> Fax 203-845-0498
> *www.scholastic.com/westonwoods*

Lesson 8

Farm Animals Series: Available in single paperback and in sets from Heinemann, 888-454-2279, or online at *heinemannclassroom.com*.